In der Sommerfrische.

Auf dem Königssee: Fahrt nach St. Bartholomä.

Zwischen Berchtesgaden und dem Königssee.

Heimkehr von einer Bergparthie.

Im Ankleidezimmer des Salinengebäudes.

Auf der Wanderung im Bergwerk.

Ausfahrt aus dem Bergwerk.

important sector of Berchtesgaden's economy. The guest's overnight accommodations rose from 300,000 in 1949 to 3 million in 1983. Whereas in the 1950s special trains constituted the main means of transportation, the mechanization in the 1960s made the guests mobile to an extent the landscape of Berchtesgaden could hardly manage. Skiing had become a mass sport so that the disclosure of the area by cable railway, lifts and pistes had to follow. For this reason the parliament of Bavaria confirmed long-cherished plans in 1974 to change the wildlife sanctuary around the Königssee into a natio-

Top:
Guests in an open-air restaurant.

Centre: The first post car driving from Berchtesgaden to Lake Hintersee. The picture out of a newspaper was taken in 1907 in front of the Berchtesgaden station.

Bottom: The first skiers on the 'Vorder brand' in 1907. The pioneers of alpine had only ski-pole and wore normal vestment, women even skirts

Voderbrand
1907

nal park and to use the land around the old collegiate church as an alpine park. The purpose is to protect the still remaining multiform, polymorphic and peculiar landscape and to enrich the tourism by a comprehensive educational system.

Here to wheel comes full circle following the tradition of those who toured this area in the 19th century because of its scenic beauties. May the wish written on an old Berchtesgaden boundary stone 'Pax intrantibus et inhabitantibus', 'Peace be unto the visitors and the inhabitants' come true for all those who live in this marvellously beautiful country and those who visit it.

Top: Postcard around the turn of the century, a view taken from the 'Malerhügel'. Beneath the 'Stiftskirche' (collegiate church) the local brewery and the alley leading to the salt mine.

Bottom: Berchtesgaden, seen from the 'Lockstein' around 1880. The former castle garden which today serves as spa garden lies between the castle with the collegiate church and the 'Franziskanerkirche'.

Market Berchtesgaden

By reason of the limited ppulation and nutrition basis only two bigger settlements respectively markets emerged in the Berchtesgaden area: Berchtesgaden and Marktschellenberg.

Berchtesgaden, the village of foundation and of the greatest importance, is situated more or less like a cell nucleus in the midst of the country supplying it and which is supplied by it in return, a bit elevated in the centre of a basin that concerning the traffic conditions is very favourable as it combines all important valleys, watercourses and arterial roads. The first churches, inns and small shops were founded here and later on replaced by guesthouses and enterprises.

The fact that the market has never been fortified ist characteristic of the centre's peculiarity, although Lockstein und Kälberstein could easily have served as hills for fortress and protection. The reason for that is the fact that Berchtesgaden owes its rise to the foundation of a monastery, was dominated by the church for centuries and has never tried to expand outwards. In addition to that, the Berchtesgadeners protected by mighty massifs obviously felt sure enough. So the town wall followed the natural passes and glens.

The market place and the Nonntal grew together so close that they soon formed an inseparable complex unity, courtly, residence-like, in alpine rococo, but not urban. The biggest part of this historic face has been preserved and today people try to adapt necessary renovations to the old picture of the town. The Federal Office for the preservation of historical monuments has promulgated a proposal for the renovation and colouration of the houses, which step by step ist being complied with.

The 'market', meaning the centre, occupies a strong position in the native population's thinking, for the tourists it is an excellent setting-off point and central point. Berchtesgaden is the seat of the authorities, here you find the spa direction, the spa garden and the kurhaus, the castle and the museum of local history and geography, the railway station and the bus terminal and not least hotels, restaurants and cafés. The centre has its effects on the show business as well with concerts of the spa orchestra, peasant theatre, cinema and performances in the Kur- and Kongreßhaus.

For pedestrians Berchtesgaden is not an easy, but instead an extraordinary village. A little reminiscence of the South is obvious, the houses with their gardens laid out in terraces cling to the steep hills. The roads are narrow, winding, their passage demands precaution. No house, however, is squeezed so much that it would not offer a view, no corner is so narrow that it would not be reached by the picture of the mountains. This central situation gives Berchtesgaden many possibilities for walks, excursions, hikings, drives and tours and each one of the neighbouring communities can be reached within a short time.

Berchtesgaden
and its places of interest

The development of tourism

There was not yet a single sign of tourism when the goods from Berchtesgaden, »Berchtolsgadener Waare«, were known as popular articles in Cadiz, Antverp and all important ports as well as for example in Augsburg, Nuremberg or Vienna. The »Berchtolsgadener Waare« comprised wooden boxes, cases, wooden tools, carvings, animals of any kind, dolls and toys, crucifixes, pictures of saints, rosaries, clock cases and thousands of other things. These products of folk art and folkcraft did not come from an unimportant small market town, but from one of the Papal States the princely provosts of which were even authorized to participate in the Emperor's election as German princes. The Berchtesgaden industry of wooden articles went through its most flourishing time in the 17th century. At that time there were places of business in all European commercial centres.

For centuries the pilgrimages had been a sort of precursor of the present tourism. As nobody knew the notion of holiday in today's sense people went for several days on a pilgrimage to well-known places like Kunterweg, St. Bartholomä, Ettenberg and Maria Gern. These pilgrims were accomodated and taken care of in the neighbouring inns, so the first accommodation places came into being.

The beginning of the 19th century saw the origins of holiday traffic which had nothing to do with pilgrimage any more, but served pleasure, the artistic contemplation of beauties of nature or the zeal for research. As a result of this scientific research and alpine disclosure Berchtesgaden became known to wider circles by means of innumerable descriptions of the journey. Other things supervened, the road conditions in the Berchtesgaden valley basin for instance were fundamentally improved from 1806 to 1810 when Berchtesgaden after an almost 700-year-long sovereignty immediately came to Austria. In 1810 Berchtesgaden came to Bavaria and in the follo-

Postcard around the turn of the century with' greetings form Berchtesgaden'.

Ottmar Ziener, München

GRUSS aus BERCHTESGADEN.

Hôtel-Pension Bahnhof.

wing decades the Bavarian royal house of Wittelsbach chose the area to be their summer residence and court hunting ground. Therefore, Berchtesgaden became more and more known, attracting artists of high reputation like Schinkel, Olivier, Waldmüller, Reinhold, Schlotterbeck, Rottmann, Carolsfeld. Their pictures and illustrations of scenic beauties aroused the desire of many of the observers to see the landscape around the Watzmann with their own eyes.

During the second half of the 19th century the railway gradually spread over Europe promoting the inclination to travel to an unimagined extent, the foundation of the Alpine mountaineering club being one of the consequences as well. Every section of the Alpine club took charge of certain groups of mountains and the construction of huts and paths there. When in 1888 Berchtesgaden was within reach by train tourism in today's sense was born. Prince Regent Luitpold of Bavaria, Princess Terese of Bavaria, Duke Schaumburg-Lippe, Archduchess Adelgunde of Austria and Grand Duke Paul of Russia represented the élite of the royal persons staying longer every year.

The boarding-house Moritz on the Obersalzberg enjoyed busy popularity. Ludwig Ganghofer, Peter Rossegger, Professor Dr. Carl von Linde, the inventor of the liquefacion of air and relatives of the Bavarian, Austrian and Prussian royal houses were among its true frequentors. So a fundamental structural change was within a good century caused by tourism and the come-and-go of the summer-holiday-makers.

The basis of existence of seven and a half centuries, namely salt production, woodworking and the transport of these goods to the customers more and more paled into insignificance. This change towards tourism as the source of income naturally had a certain influence upon the tradition-conscious way of life, especially upon the deeply rooted customs and traditional costumes. But this pop up of tourism contributed for instnce to the preservation of the beautiful traditional costumes as one becomes conscious of quick changes more easily than of slow-acting ones. The foundation of the Christmas Rifle Clubs and the Society for the continued use of costumes occured in the time between the two World Wars. After World War II tourism developed to the most

Top: Prince Regent Luitpold von Bayern (1821-1912) was a great patron and benefactor of Berchtesgaden and an enthusiast friend of the area. Every year mostly in autumn, he took residence in the castle for enjoying hunts in this area. After the death ot the ill-minded King Louis II Prince Regent Luitpold took over the regency in 1886 as also King Louis' brother Otto suffered from that illness and could by no means take over power.

Centre: Drivers during one of the numerous huntings in the time of the Prince Regent.

Bottom: Crown Prince Rupprecht von Bayern (1869-1955) in Berchtesgaden.

Right page: Pictures from Berchtesgaden and its surroundings, drawings from 1880.

From the Lockstein we have an impressive view of the city of Berchtesgaden towered above by the all-dominating Watzmann which — like the Matterhorn in Zermatt/Switzerland — has become the landmark of Berchtesgaden.

Top: Berchtesgaden, seen from the inn 'Salzbergalm'. In the centre you see the collegiate church with the two steeples and the long-stretched out former convent buildings which became the summer residence of the royal house of the Wittelsbacher in 1893 after the secularization. On the left side a cable car of the 'Obersalzbergbahn' leading up to the Obersalzberg road in two zones.

Bottom: The octagonal market fountain in the middle of the 'Marktplatz'. It was built for the 50th anniversary of Berchtesgaden's affiliation to Bavaria. Already in 1558 a wooden fountain was at the same place which served as watering place. It was, as tells the inscription on this picure as well, rebuilt in marble in 1677.

Right page, top: Children of the society for the continued use of traditional costumes during a celebration on the market place when several dances and 'Schuhplattler' are performed by the tradition-conscious societies.

Right page, bottom: Japanese cherry trees in blossom in the Berchtesgaden spa garden which is open to everybody. During the season the spa orchestra plays popular melodies in the afternoon, furthermore a garden café invites to stay a little longer.

points of interest
in the Market Berchtesgaden

The market place, having preserved its old face, shows traditional, alpine buildings.

The big corner house opposite the market fountain, once called 'House at the bridge', afterwards called 'House of the Stag' is dated 1594, but was reconstructed several times.

Its Southern side is covered by Renaissance frescoes, painted around 1600 and showing parodying monkey scenes, the oldest profane house paintings in the South German area. Not far away from the market place we find the 'Hotel Post', the former 'Leithaus' which is the oldest inn in Berchtesgaden, already mentioned in 1328, reconstructed in 1984. At the market place itself we find the restaurant 'Neuhaus' which was built in 1576, the second eldest inn which was renovated in 1971. We find well-preserved guestrooms on the first floor. An archway connects the 'Neuhaus' and the old 'Kornmesserhaus', another archway leads further to the castle. In 1978 a pedestrian zone was created between the market place and the kurhaus.

Whereas the market place demonstrates a cheerful traditional charakter, the castle place still today represents the courtly, residence-like character of the former clerical princedom. This spacious place impresses by its compactness: the dignity of the 'Stiftskirche' (collegiate church), the castle's façade in elegant ornamental plasterwork and the arcades of the former royal stud are a great background.

The collegiate church dominates the castle place, it was built in Roman style in the 12th century, extended in the 13th century by an early Gothic gallery and went through several alterations. The sacristy keeps a precious silver altar and a liturgical vestment offered by Maria Teresia. Next to the church we find the royal castle, once used as residence of the prince bishops. The castle is the result of a building activity lasting for centuries which because of the secularization was finished at the western wing in 1803. At that time it came to the Wittelsbachers, the Bavarian royal house. Owing to the initiative of Crown Prince Rupprecht (1869-1955) the princely rooms built in Gothic to late rococo style were put in a dignified state. When entering the castle for visiting it one has to see the late Roman cloister, the oldest well-preserved monument of Berchtesgaden. On the floor we find ledgers of former prince bishops and canons, the small inner court is filled with an atmosphere of silence and engrossment.

The entrance to the castle is formed by the dormitory of the monks, an elegant, late Gothic hall. The former convent rooms with exquisite Renaissance furniture and baroque appointments follow in a long row. In the dining-room a table is laid with Nymphenburg porcelaine, another suite keeps a collection of German Romanticists' paintings. The tour ends on a garden terrace where a small rose garden contains a Florentine fountain and together with the mountains an impression of special beauty arises.

Left, top and centre: Scenes from a performance in the peasant theatre. The play 'Father's Day' is performed when two fathers have to learn by many involvements and funny situations that their wives' children whom they had considered to be illegitimate were theirs. We will not say any more, watch the play yourself.

Left, bottom: Historic kitchen with an open smoke outlet and a hook for the cauldron to be seen in the museum of local history and culture in 'Schloß Adelsheim'. This museum is one of Bavaria's most important, non-governmental museums.

Right page: View of Berchtesgaden covered in deep snow from the 'Soleleitungsweg' which clings to the mountains above Berchtesgaden and offers marvellous views of the village and the surrounding mountains. This picture is directed towards the 'Obersalzberg', 'Oberau' and the 'Roßfeld'.

In the museum of local history and geography in Schloß Adelsheim, a representative building in late Renaissance, everything once valid in Berchtesgaden has been registered. Many of the exhibits remind us of the former Augustinian canon convent, as well as of the Bavarian royal house, the bourgeoisie, the former peasant life and historic traditional costumes.

Finally a shop for Berchtesgaden artistic articles of handicraft is situated in this museum. This multiple and often-cited folkcraft could be preserved in many branches. One finds the typical Berchtesgaden Spanschachteln (boxes of wood shavings) in all sizes, forms and paintings, beyond that toys, wooden plates, candle sticks, fumigating men, peasant candle-carrying angels, butter moulds, so-called carriages of sovereignity, stars of wood shavings, wax figures, ceramics and original Christmas tree decoration. In no case you should miss a visit there and perhaps you should buy this or that souvenir.

Another point of interest is the Franziskanerkirche (Franciscan church), once called Frauenkirche am Anger (women's chuch next to the village green), a hall of two naves from the 16th century with a late Gothic net vault. At the Northern side of this church we find the old Berchtesgaden graveyard, beneath the steeple the grave of the merchant Anton Adner (1705-1822). Adner was a boxmaker who as a traveller sold his products outside Berchtesgaden as well. He carried his carvings in a knapsack, a statue in the museum of local history and geogranphy shows him as traveller, knitting socks what once was an activity of Berchtesgaden's men.

A visit to the peasant theatre is interesting and amusing as well. Already in the 18th century there was the theatre with peasants who liked acting as leading men. At the beginning it was probably dialogues of persons from the Bible, then plays of more dialogues with colourful sets and stages. More and more worldly scenes mingled with the religious story. At that time dramas of witches, robbers and knights were very popular. Only the beginning tourism at the turn of the century featured comedy, burlesque and merry tales. So Berchtesgaden's peasant theatre was founded at that time, it was usually played in hotels and inns, and today it ist the only German peasant theatre that owns a proper house. Film, radio and television became aware of this theatre and so already more than 10 performances were shown on tv, and the tenth will never be the last one. The repertory comprises plays like 'The farm shying away from girls', 'Grandpa does stupidities', 'The three saints of the village', 'The wooden virgin', 'Marriage fever' and 'Father's Day'.

Lake Königssee

View from the Malerwinkel across the silent lake early in the morning. The centre of the picture where the lake seems to end shows the church of St. Bartholomä. Above that, the pointed pyramid of the Schönfeldspitze, on the left side the huge block of the Funtenseetauern lying in the sunlight. Already in the 19th century this fascinating panorama attracted artists from all over Europe and their works have essentially contributed to make crossing the lake the peak of a visit to Berchtesgaden.

Below: Return after ski hiking on the Steinernes Meer. At the end the steep course of old snow leads across the Sagerecker path down to Lake Königssee. In the opposite direction (little picture) the lake looks pleasantly embedded between the foothills of the Watzmann on the left side and the Gotzenberge on the right side.

Top: The hotel 'Schiffmeister' and the boats' landing-stage at the Northern end of the lake. Here used to be the boat's huts which today are East of the boat's landing-stage. The form of these huts goes back to a historic style which can be seen on pictures of the early 19th century. On the 12th June 1918 all huts and a part of the hotel were destroyed by the flames, later on reconstructed following the historic drawings of August Thiersch.

Right, top: A new boat on Lake Königssee, the 'Grün-stein' was consecrated in 1958 and put to service. It should be mentioned here that the national shipping society on Lake Königssee has its own shipyard here and repairs the boats or even constructs new ones in winter.

Left, bottom: Still today long flat boats are being used the so-called 'Landauer' which were the only means of transportation on Lake Königssee for centuries.

Shipping on the Königssee

For the disclosure of the pathless mountains around the Königssee and the Obersee shipping played a special role. For centuries the traditional rowing boats were the only means of transportation on the Königssee, those typical flat boats which still today are being used. Larger flat boats, the so-called 'Landauer' were used for pilgrimages and similar things. As the Königssee attracted more and more visitors a steam-driven motorboat should relieve the shipping on the Königssee in 1873. But that project was dropped as coal firing was impossible because of the pollution of the water. Furthermore, King Louis II owing to his romantic imaginations did not to want know anything of the technicalization of shipping, at least on the Königssee. After tedious tests the first electric boat approved by the Prince Regent crossed the lake in July 1909. It was driven by accumulator batteries and therefore it was quite silent. The visitors preferred these electric boats to the tradi-

15

Left, top: View of the majestic silent 'Königssee' from the 'Archenkanzel'. From here the path 'Rinnkendlsteig' leads down to St. Bartholomä, a tour that is recommendable to expert alpinists.

Geographic situation and particularity

tional flat boats and the so-called 'Landauer'. Today the fleet on Königssee consists of more than 21 boats whose names remind us of mountain, lakes and villages in the Berchtesgaden area. In summer boat crossings start early in the morning and end in the late afternoon.

Intermediate crossings are made if need be and so the punctual transportation of the guests even during the peak tourist season can be guaranteed. The crossings can be interrupted in St. Bartholomä and in Salet. Shipping is done throughout the year and is only stopped if the lake is iced over.

Lake Königssee lies embedded like a fiord between the Watzmann, the Hagengebirge and the Steinernes Meer (Stony Sea). Its shore is precipitous and the rock faces tower up no less steep around the lake. The narrow, long-stretched-out form of the lake's basin catches our eyes at once, its length measures 4.78 miles, its widest breadth 0.74 mile only. With a surface of 2 square miles it is one of Bavaria's smaller lakes, but due to its depth of 164 yards it is one of Middle Europe's deepest lakes. With that Lake Königssee widely differs from the rest of Bavaria's lakes which without exception are situated in the flat, hilly Alpine foothills, having developed under the influence of the last Ice Age 12.000 years ago. Lake Königssee's basin, however, developed 140 million years before owing to a graben that was only deepened by the following Ice Age. Due to two characteristics it is

the only of 25 Bavarian lakes that has not yet been damaged.

First of all, its fiord-like embedding between the rock faces and the mountain slopes prevents any construction of roads and buildings around the lake.

Secondly, the position in high mountains of its catchment basin, that means that part of the region where all surface and underground waters come from, ensures the inflow of crystal-clear water. 64 % of this catchment basin consist of plant coverings, 28 % are covered by forests and 8 % represent alpine meadows; the water flowing off is free from any substances with which to-day's industrial society strains almost all the running waters of its settlement area. Life at Lake Königssee has not been disturbed, as the lake has preserved its ecologist balance; under these circumstances it has remained

Top: View from the 'Feuerpalfen' near the 'Gotzenalm' of the peninsula of St. Bartholomä and the Watzmann's Eastern rock face. The peninsula was formed in the course of thousands of years by the 'Eisbach' uninterruptedly transporting stones and debris out of the 'Eisbachtal'. Above the Eastern rock face you see the 'Mittelspitze', the Watzmann's highest elevation, left of it the 'Südspitze' and right of it the 'Hocheck'.

a natural lake and with it the centre of the National Park Berchtesgaden.

Top: The world-famous buildings on St. Bartholomä, namely the church, the fisher's house and the shipyard.

Left: The impressive wooden altar in barock of the church of St. Bartholomä. The altar-panel shows the martyr of Saint Bartholomew and was painted by the court painter Johann Degler from Munich.

Points of interest around Lake Königssee

The shipyards of the national shipping company at the shore go back to a historic structure within the 19th century and were reconstructed after their complete destruction by a fire in 1918. Near the shipyards we find the isle of Christlieger. The boats pass its Western side, in former times they used to pass the other side, a narrow place between the shore and the isle. On the isle we find a statue of Saint Nepomuk which according to an old oral tradition was built up after the saving of shipwrecked persons in 1711. In the romantic 19th century the idyllic situation incited people to arrange the isle artitstically and to lay out an English garden that today does no longer exist. In a small creek at the North-Eastern side of the lake we find the place called Malerwinkel with its world-famous view across the lake's surface to St. Bartholomä. This panorama was appreciated, often dessigned and painted by the painters and graphic artists of Romanticism.

On a vertical rock of the mighty Falkensteinwand opposite the Malerwinkel we discover a stone cross with an inscription. This spot reminds us of the sinking of a boat carrying pilgrims in 1688 when these pilgrims from Maria Alm drowned during a thunderstorm. The Chronicles report: 'On the 23rd August, 1688, when many people went on a pilgrimage across the mountains to St. Bartholomä, the boat sank and seventy persons drowned'. The echo signifies a certain spot on the lake between the Königsbachfall (Königsbach waterfall) and Kessel, where the echo is reverberated several times. Today the echo is produced by blowing a rural melody on the trumpet, whereas in former times several gun salutes were fired. In the 19th century the so-called Kessel at the Eastern side of the lake was a very popular place for the Berchtesgadeners. It owes its popularity to the view of St. Bartholomä and the wild and romantic gorge of the Kesselbach. In the fashion of the 19th century, an English garden was laid out here as well and a hermit chapel, the so-called pilgrims' hermitage was built, too. By this close combination of nature, art, religion and philosophy the Kessel became an important witness of Romanticism at Lake Königssee. St. Bartholomä is situated on a peninsula deposited by the Eisbach, the so-called meadow land of Bartholomä. The pilgrimage church and the former castle dominate the unity of construction here. Together they form a homogeneous main body of building. The single-nave church has been erected with a constructionally luxurious arrangement of three semi-domes, that is the ground plan shows a quadrate centre and three equal semi-domes in the form of a clover-leaf at three sides of it. The former hunting seat can be recognized in spite of many changes during the 20th century and today it serves as restaurant with rural character. In addition to that this building unity comprises the 'Fischerhaus' (fishers' house), the shipyards, the 'Meierhof' (dairy farmer's farm) and the 'Jägerhaus' (hunters' house).

The Ice Chapel signifies a glacial gate at the foot of the Watzmann's Eastern rock face formed by the Eisbach from a névé field.

This névé field is the lowest of the Eastern Alps. During the time of Romanticism a visit to the Ice Chapel used to be the peak of shipping on Lake Königssee.

Top: Dramatic view of the Watzmann's Eastern rock face after a sudden change of weather in the early summer. Such situations cost the lives of many people crossing the face, especially by rockfall, undercooling and avalanches. An icy avalanche is to be seen on the left upper side of the picture.

Bottom: The so-called 'Eiskapelle' (ice chapel) formed by the 'Eisbach' under the edge of the avalanche. In 1983 it broke down and buried a group of pupils. Two pupils were killed.

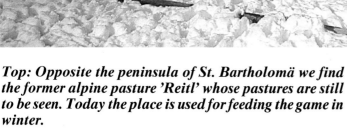

Top: Opposite the peninsula of St. Bartholomä we find the former alpine pasture 'Reitl' whose pastures are still to be seen. Today the place is used for feeding the game in winter.

South of St. Bartholomä we find the rock face Burgstall-wand, famous for the former 'dry wood fall', when high at the top of the rock wood was stacked up and put at safe by a barrier. At certain times the wood was launched into the lake, where it was collected and finally pulled to the Northern end of the lake. South-East of Lake Königssee we find Lake Obersee separated from the latter only by a narrow strip of land resulting from a landslide.

In the background we see the two 'Teufelshörner' (devil's horns) towering above the serious and deserted lake. The Röthbachfall comes down from the Röth to Fischunkel which is the backmost, godforsaken corner.

Bottom: Rest after a walk across the frozen lake. This event is only possible a few times within a generation. After 17 years the lake was frozen-over again in 1980/81 fortunately again 1981/82 and two years later in 1984/85. It is not astonishing that everyone takes the opportunity to cross the lake either on foot, bicycle, sled or cross-country skis.

Let's say another word about the front-page nature and environment protection: In 1978 the alpine and national park Lake Königssee was set up by a decree of the Bavarian government. With its surface of some 55893.1

acres (20035.925 square miles) the national park approximately corresponds to the former nature reserve around Lake Königssee. It is the Southern part of the big alpine park of Berchtesgaden with a total surface of 113670.6 acres (43888.218 square miles).

The landscape of the national park is marked by the massifs of Reiteralm, Hochkalter, Watzmann, Steinernes Meer, Hagengebirge and Hoher Göll together with Hohes Brett. The three deeply cut in valleys of Lake Königssee, the Wimbach and the Klausbach underline the division of the massifs. The surface in front of the alpine park is also called the 'approaches' or foothills.

These approaches comprise the inhabited regions of the communities of Markt Berchtesgaden, Marktschellenberg, Schönau am Königssee, Ramsau and Bischofswiesen as well as the massifs of Untersberg and Lattengebirge. The national park wants to leave nature to itself,

Top:
Lake Königssee not yet fully frozen-over in 1980/1981.

explore nature and communicate to man the natural beauties and their correlations with nature. If you visit the national park around Lake Königssee, please contribute to the protection of nature and environment by not leaving the marked paths, not being noisy, not disturbing the animals, not tearing off any plants and taking your rubbish back home again.

Don't forget to visit the national park's information bureau in the old Königssee station, either. Here you can watch either a diatone film about the aim and object of the national park or video films about various topics, as for instance about rock goats, chamoises or mountain maple. Questions will be replied by an expert assistant who will also propose various walks in the national park.

Top and bottom: In former times Lake Königssee was of special importance for the alpine pastures as the inaccessible mountains could easily be disclosed after the transportation on the lake. The pastures lying on the lake were 'Ronner', 'Kessel', 'Reitl', 'Salet' and 'Fischunkel' which connects Lake Königssee and Lake Obersee.

When being driven to or from the alpine pastures the cattle is transported on the 'Landauer'. The 'Grafelbauer' from the Obersalzberg who runs the 'Fischunkelalm' decorates his cows after a summer without any accidents with the so-called 'Fuikln' when he has arrived at the village of Königssee and then goes to the usual stable with the cattle's noise of the bells.

In a report around the turn of the century one can read: 'Girls in full array accompany their decorated brown cattle with the white back. But of course only if no misfortune has happened to the farmer and his herd... for the same number of cattle shall come back from the alpine pastures as have been driven to. Many rosettes have to be bound by the alpine dairymaids for one bull alone carries a 'Fuikl' of 200 of them'.

Right page, top: Aerial photograph showing the remote part of Lake Königssee and Lake Obersee, the landing-stage and the path connecting the two lakes. The 'Röth' towers up beyond Lake Obersee and the two 'Teufelshörner' are it tops.

Still very interesting is the fact that the German office of national parks within the scope of its research works together with the biologist Dr. Fricke who made it his duty to explore the deep alpine lakes. He has already done several dives in the lakes Mondsee, Traunsee, the notorious Toplitzsee and in Lake Königssee in 1983 with his little submarine GEO.

During the dives in Lake Königssee he stopped his submarine on the deepest spot of about 202.3 yards, discovered strange rings on the bottom which turned out to be traces of an earthworm-like animal nothing is known about by now. Furthermore, strange little craters were discovered and those uniformly arranged structures are supposed to be gas pockets whose gas is formed by rotten leaves and escapes through the hole.

Besides phantastic reefs from shells having died off more than 190 millions of years ago man's waste was found as well, for example near a debris cone off St. Bartholomä lots of rubbish, boxes and cases were found.

Several corpses were found on the bottom of the lake as well, for instance that of the Berchtesgadener who in 1963 wanted to cross the frozen lake with his VW, but broke through the ice near the Falkensteiner Wand and sank.

Having finished his divings, Dr. Fricke came to the conclusion that Lake Königssee is the cleanest and most healthy in the Alps what not at least is due to the uninhabited shore.

Visiting the
salt mine of Berchtesgaden

When Berchtesgaden still was in the hands of the prince-provosts only chosen people were allowed to visit the salt mine. Today this mine is open to everybody who wants to enter it in the protecting clothing of all miners that already kings and princes had to wear. Visiting this mine running normally is especially fascinating and completely harmless.

A mine railway takes us 656 yards into the mountain to the Kaiser-Franz-Sinkwerk. An easy stair-way and a slide polished by innumerous miners' trousers lead further down to the experimental pit on the deepest spot of the mine. Now we have 4 strata, drifts, shafts, ways and galleries constructed centuries ago above ourselves. We pass a grotto where the transparent colourfulness of the salt is magically reflected, and continue to go deeper into the mountain.

Having passed time-honoured marble tablets telling of of the openings of new pits, we come right into the present, to a cinema. Here, films are shown about the evolution of these enormous salt deposits and how their salt

is produced. The peak of this underground tour is a voyage on a safe raft over a salt lake which is about 109 yards long and 33 yards wide and with that is one of the largest pits in the world. At the shore the ancient underground means of transportation, a slide, awaits us and by the mine railway we come back to daylight again.

The production of salt and the saltworks (F. Hofmann)

The underground workings of this salt mine are based on four adit levels (strata). Three of the adits are separated from each other by 27-yard-thick walls. A 16.3-yard-thick wall separates King-Louis' adit from the adit called Ferdinandsberg. In the depth of 65 yards, beneath King-Louis' adit (valley bottom), the deep mining bottom has been begun by constructing a blind pit which will soon be put into operation.

The oldest process known to us is the winning of salt-water in a bucket elevator where the freshwater after its enrichment with salt is scooped out. We have, however, no information about size and output of these elevators. This type of mining practised for centuries is the classical type of mining in the Alps. For centuries it was considered to be the only method of winning salt from the

'Haselgebirge', a mixture of salt, clay and anhyride. As there is no salt occuring in its pure form as rock-salt and cannot simply be dynamited, passed through a sieve and packed up, it first has to be extracted from the rocks by means of freshwater and then be turned to salt by the evaporation of the water. So-called 'artistic constructions' are necessary for that.

Left page, bottom: The salt mine is visited in the costumes of the salt miners the pit railway being used for coming in or getting off.

Right, top: The councillor of the salt mine and saltworks Georg von Reichenbach who in 1817/18 constructed the saltwater pipe line Berchtesgaden - Reichenhall.

Right, bottom: Entry to the 'Frauenberg' pit that was opened in 1559.

For the construction of the first pits an adit inclined of 40 degrees was built making it possible to come to the 32-yard-deep beginning of the new workshop which was to be excaved by hand by means of devices similar to those of ore miners. Rock was carried through this gallery and later on the water line was fitted in. At last, a dam was built by using the rocks of a closed down pit. Through this dam the saltwater was conducted through a pipe line fastened there. It sometimes happened that the dam leaked or even broke. Only the building of another gallery where water is conducted and the saltwater won is drained of this constant source of danger has been removed.

The construction of a modern pit is carried out as follows: Starting from the main shaft a gallery is caved about 49 yards into the field dessignated by the mining surveyors. From here another shaft is put down following the enlargement of the first pit. At the end the workshop is installed with 32-yard-long vertical ways upwards at both sides. Rectangular cross-connections of 16 yards are added. So a workshop of the length of 65 yards, the width of 38 yards and the height of 2.2 yards is made.

In former times the dynamited Haselgebirge was carried by means of buckets to an already shut down pit. Here it was disintegrated and turned into saltwater. A sieve of 1.2 square yards consisting of square timbers mounted like venetian blinds serves to pump clay and anhydrites. With the pump, the lines for saltwater and freshwater being installed the pit's construction is finished.

This chamber then is filled with frehswater. Everyday the water lixiviates about 0.4 inches of the saltern rocks. The unnecessary components sink to the bottom. Anyhydrites remain as rocks. The waste sinking to the bottom forms an impermeable layer. About 130 cubic yards of salt water of 26,5 % are produced per day. The filling in of freshwater must be carried out so that highly concentrated saltwater can be produced by lixiviating and not too much saltwater is pumped because in both cases the saturation point would by likely to sink.

Left, top: Miners after working in front of the Ferdinandsberg' pit.

Left, bottom:
The miners of Berchtesgaden in 1923.

Bottom:
Drawing of a standard bearer in a parade.

On an average, those pits are exploited for about ten years. During that time about 392.000 cubic yards of saturated saltwater are won.

Since 1975 salt water winning in drilling chambers has been developed. This type of mining has replaced the classical type. By central drillings and their specified geological evalution the spot of a pit is determined to exclude any premature end of production. Already when working on the underground pit the most modern machines are being used. From a drilling chamber a hole of a diameter of 26 inches is drilled 136 yards into the depth. Filling in freshwater and the transportation of the unnecessary rocks make up a funnel-like cavity of 4,577 to 6,535 cubic yards. This cavity is permanently filled with freshwater. The difference between the classical type of salt mining and this type is that no longer a lake of salt water, but a cylindric shaft is being exploited.

This new type of mining, for the first time developed in the salt mine of Berchtesgaden, is more efficient, saves working time and offers a better exploitation of the salt deposits.

Boiling of the saltwater is done in the saltworks in Bad Reichenhall where it finally becomes table salt. A modern saltwater line connects the saltworks with the mine via Hallthurm. This line was put into operations in 1961 and replaces the old line via Wachterl built by Reichenbach in 1817. Already in 1555, the saltworks 'Frauenreuth' situated where today we find the station of Bad Reichenhall boiled saltwater and turned it into table salt.

A historic boiling works consisted of the brewing room and contained a rectangular warming pan of about 140 square yards and a circular granulator pan of 307 square yards.

The granulator pan was fired by wood and its heat warmed up the warming pan made up of cast iron plates and equipped with a wooden fume hood. The granulator pan was fabricated from double-clinched iron sheets and lay on fireproof stands. At the same time the whole pan was hung on the roof timbers by means of strong hooks.

The fire room consisted of 10 horizontal arches built in brick, were 1.9 yards long separated from the next by 1.9 yards and formed the fire grate. The pans themselves were covered by a light wooden roof. The saltwater of 26.7 % flew out of the containers through cast iron pipes, was heated up to 68 to 86 degrees Fahrenheit and then flew into the warming pan. There it was heated almost to its boiling point so that calcium carbonate was as so-called warming stone to be found on the pan's bottom.

From this warming pan the developing salt was brought to the granulator pan. There the coarse-grained salt was extracted. The remaining substances having developed by the permanent evaporation and extraction of the salt is replaced by new salt water coming in from the warming pan. Every two hours the salt was extracted by means of wooden tools (crutches) to a small basin where the saltwater won could flow in.

Top:
The peak of a visit in the salt mine is driving over the salt-lake on a raft. This salt lake is one of Europe's largest salt lakes.

Right page, bottom left:
In a crosscut we find one of the two water column hoisting devices built up by Reichenbach in 1817 for the salt water pipe line to Bad Reichenhall.

Right page, bottom right:
Cabinet of the salt mine's minerals.

Wooden forms equipped with iron rings, the so-called 'Bärkufen' were standing on a wooden groyne. They were filled with wet salt and usually consisted of a cut skittle of about 0.12 cubic yards. Afterwards the forms were turned upside down on the groyne, so that the still remaining saltwater could flow off. In so-called dehydrating upfolds, 8 in number in the salt-works 'Frauenreuth', they were dried.

In 1920 the saltworks 'Frauenreuth' was closed down.

29

Obersalzberg – Adolf Hitler

In an altitude of 3,820 feet, at the foothills of the Hoher Göll and the Kehlstein we find the Obersalzberg, a region of steep meadows, much wood and today much brush covering unfortunate ruins. What happened on the Obersalzberg?

As already the name implies the interior of the Obersalzberg covers a large rock stratum, a conglomerate which as remains of the last Ice Age contains salt that is won off the mountain by a process of leaching out. Through centuries the natives found work in the salt mine, here and there a small house was built, several meadows were wrested from the wood and it took great efforts to build up a farm here. So a loose settlement on the Obersalzberg started, here the 'Bodnerlehen', the 'Scheberlehen', 'Beim Breiler' and 'in der Brandstatt'. That's how it was for centuries.

It was not before 1877 that the first boarding house, 'Pension Moritz' was built. Peter Rossegger and Ludwig Ganghofer stopped at it, as well as the Bavarian royal house and the Austrian imperial family. Other well-known people settled here, for instance the privy councillor Carl von Linde, the inventer of the liquefaction of air, the grand-piano manufacturer Bechstein and the councillor of commerce Winter from Buxtehude. He built a small house beneath the Bodnerlehen and called it 'Haus Wachenfeld'. With this house the Obersalzberg's fate began.

After the coup of the 9 November 1923 and his imprisonment in Landsberg Adolf Hitler came to the Obersalzberg, to a little blockhouse above the 'Platterhof'. Gradually he made friends with his neighbours, friends and supporters took care of him. His sister bought 'Haus Wachenfeld'. Hitler bought it from her in 1927 as he had not been able to find another home. Everything remained as it was before, only less important alterations completed the house.

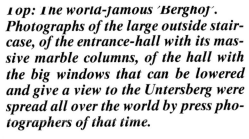

Top: The world-famous 'Berghof'. Photographs of the large outside staircase, of the entrance-hall with its massive marble columns, of the hall with the big windows that can be lowered and give a view to the Untersberg were spread all over the world by press photographers of that time.

Top: As after the assumption of power in 1933 thousands of visitors streamed up to the mountain every day, permits became necessary and the whole area was changed into the Führer zone.

Centre: Teatime on the Western side of the 'Berghof' terrace. In the background the adjutant's office.

Bottom: Hitler's office for the furniture of which only the best materials were used.

Kapelle „Maria Hilf"

Kindersanatorium Seitz

Bodnerlehen

Haus Bormann

Oberwurflehen

Gasthof zum Türken

Haus Wachenfeld (Berghof)

Villa Bechstein

Only when Hitler became Chancellor of the Reich in 1933 his household was enlarged, guests and party celebrities surrounded him, thousands of his adherents wanted to see him on the Obersalzberg and so the second alteration of the house became necessary. Hitler's secretary Rudolf Heß took up the negociations with the owners of the neighbouring pieces of land. But as the latter got other duties, Martin Bormann was entrusted with the total organization of the Obersalzberg. Bormann utilized this unique chance to worm himself into Hitler's favour. Within the shortest time he acquired 3.8 square miles around Hitler's property. A 2.18-yard-high fence marked the boundaries of the intrerior Führer zone and was guarded by Adolf Hiter's body guards. The Obersalzberg natives – as far as living in the Führer zone – were dismissed and placed into other regions of the Berchtesgaden district. The whole affair was of course not carried out without reprisals.

In 1935 the great construction fever started. 'Haus Wachenfeld' was changed into the much bigger 'Berghof' with its well-known outdoor stairs and the enormous windows of the conference room. The guesthouse 'Türken' became the control centre of the Reich's secret service and the state police and the lodgings for the bodygards were built right behind it. Goebbels took residence in 'Haus Bechstein', Hermann Göring built up a country house with a swimming pool on the beautiful 'Eckerbichl'. Martin Bormann wishing to stay close to Hitler took possession of the children's home 'Seitz' with his large family, Reichsminister Speer took over the 'Waltenbergerheim'.

Underground bunkers connected the 'Berghof' with the most important places, the self-sufficient completion was formed by the 'Gutshof', greenhouses and other supply bases. Officials and employees for all of the

Platterhof (Pension Moritz)

Moritz Dependance,
später Parteigästehaus

Gasthof Steiner

Lochnermühle

Baumgartlehen

operation were accommodated in the new settlements of 'Klaushöhe' and 'Buchenhöhe'. A new Chancellery of the Reich was as sub-branch office of Berlin's built up in Stanggaß near Berchtesgaden.

The high point of this construction activity was without any doubt the construction of the Eagle's Nest on the 6,016 feet high Kehlstein. It was Bormann's idea to ingratiate himself with Hitler by giving him this building for his 50th birthday. A road difficult to construct at that time leads through 5 tunnels and with only a single curve further to the parking lot at the height of 5577 feet beneath the top of the Kehlstein. From this parking lot a tunnel of the length of 406 feet was driven through the mountain at the end of which another shaft of 406 feet goes right into the interior of the Eagle's Nest.

Building on the Obersalzberg was continued even during the war. It was only in 1944 after the call to the »total war«

Top: The picture shows the area of the Obersalzberg around 1930. 'Haus Wachenfeld' was not yet changed into the 'Berghof' and the Platterhof still had its original form. Later on the Baumgartlehen was torn down and pig breeding was begun here. All houses around the inn 'Steiner', the 'Lochnermühle', the chapel, the fiefs of 'Bodnerlehen' and 'Oberwurflehen', the children's home 'Seitz' and the two fiefs above and beneath the 'Bechstein-Villa' were built.

that German workers were replaced by foreign ones. Considering the daily bombardments of so many German towns the attention was directed to the completion of the bunker system.

Top: A visit to the 'Führer' after the assumption of power, but before the great alterations.

Centre: Hitler's visit to the Göringhügel.

Bottom: View of the 'Hotel Türken' from Bormann's house serving as lodgings to the Reich's secret service. On the right side beneath the 'Berghof'.

In the following you will find a report of B. Frank who from 1943 to 1945 was the commander on the Obersalzberg:

'Experience with the top echelon of the 3rd Reich on the Obersalzberg... After Hitler's assumption of power his country residence on the Obersalzberg was changed into a centre of his power. The most important of his assistants settled in the neighborhood, too. That happened under oberservance of a certain order.

Even before 1933 Göring built up a modest house in the area above the 'Berghof'. Later on it became the country residence 'Göring'. Constructed in country style, equipped with exquisite building materals and precious furniture, it was, however, by no means able to catch up to the neighbouring 'Berghof'. Göring cared not to surpass the size, the representative equipment of the 'Berghof'.

With much more determination Bormann gained admission to the Obersalzberg, knowing that he would open a back door for his own pressure-group. After Rudolf Heß had due to his flight to England left his place as a party secretary to Martin Bormann, the latter interposed himself with his remarkably splendid furniture between the 'Berghof' and the country house 'Göring', that nearly disappeared behind the 'Göringhügel'. With this furniture and the bigger house Bormann succedded in driving Göring's house from its rank and in pushing it away from the centre of the power. It cannot be an incident that Bormann's estate bordered on Göring's, but had not entrance to it.

When afterwards the galleries of the bunkers were built up for these two houses as well, there was no underground connection between the air-raid shelter of Göring and that of Bormann, but there was one between the gallery of the 'Berghof' with the underground caves of the Führer and Bormann's air-raid shelter.

A third assistant succeeded as well in gaining foothold on the Obersalzberg and making his way to close circle of power: That was the rapid upstart of the minister of armament Speer. After the death of his predecessor Todt, who died in air crash in 1942, he made his first steps towards the circle of power. Nevertheless, the Führer zone remained limited for him. He settled down at the lowest part of the prohibited zone, near the access road to the Obersalzberg... This country residence, a reconstructed villa with a studio, was built during a phase of the war when the first crises were rankling'.

Concerning a meeting with Hitler at the end of May 1944 B. Frank reports: 'I had to do with the burden ot the newly realized fact that Hitler is a seriously ill man who at least temporarily does not have his own body in his power. I utilized every possibility of my position to learn more about Hitler's physical condition'.

At that time he acted under the influence of injections given to him regularly. They caused euphoric moods, as much as I could recognise on Hitler's birthday, which then were followed by an all the more deep decline ot his physical and psychical abilities.

He did not seem to be up to the nervous strains of carrying on war. Strong stimulants had to help. They undermined his substance. Hitler's physical condition got so bad that the architect's drawings had to be harmonized with his needs. The entrances had to be built without any stairs. Going up the stairs must have been very hard for him.

Top: 'Haus Bormann' seen from the road above the 'Hotel Türken'.

Centre: The country house 'Göring' with the swimming pool on the 'Göringhügel'.

Bottom: The 'Platterhof', bombed-down, but temporarirly repaired later on.

Top: American members of the occupation forces in the chimney room of the conquered Eagle's Nest.

Centre: General Eisenhower in the Eagle's Nest on the 2nd September 1945.

Bottom: American soldiers on the large outdoor stairs.

Right page, top: The Eagle's Nest was to be Bormann's present for Hitler's 50th birthday. In winter, the house beneath the 6026-feet-high top of the Kehlstein is cut off from the valley and is open from mid-May after the extensive and thorough cleaning of the rocks following the removal of ice and snow.

On the 25th April 1945 American aircrafts bombed the Obersalzberg in two waves, the destructions were considerable, the 'Berghof' and all other surface buildings were severely hit, but the bunkers in which some 3500 people seeked refuge were firm enough to withstand. At that time Göring had been on the Obersalzberg and as he did no longer consider Hitler in Berlin to be sound of mind, he made his world-known wireless message that he as the representative of Hitler would be willing to end the war at least against the Western Powers by all means. After that Hitler gave the instruction to arrest Göring and to remove him from all of his duties and competences. Afterwards he was brought to the village of Mauterndorf in Austria, where he finally was discovered by the Allies. His wife flew to South Tyrol (Northern Italy) with their children. The SS units marched off without a fight and the SS administration was dissolved, leaving 17 million Reichsmark of construction debts. Towards the evening of the 6th May American troups of the 101st US-Airborn division occupied the Obersalzberg. The area was torn up and strewn with bomb craters, a lunar landscape, a chaos. During the following years hardly anything changed, the Americans had occupied the area on Obersalzberg and any attempts of former inhabitants to settle down on the Obersalzberg were refused. In 1952 the Bavarian government got the permit to abrade all of the still existing ruins and bunkers. It caused a lot of trouble for the native political representatives to keep the not-bombed-out and still intact Eagle's Nest.

Since then decades have passed, during the summer months tens of thousands of tourists come to the Obersalzberg, visit the Eagle's Nest and search through the ruins and fragments of an unfortunate time. Wouldn't it be time to build up again this delightful holiday resort instead of letting it grow wild under grass and brush?

The Watzmann

The legendary Watzmann is enthroned above the valley basin of Berchtesgaden. The legend tells us:

'A long, long time ago, King Waze reigned violently over his subiects in the Berchtesgaden area. He despised any good, only loved hunting and his subjects trembled when they heard the noise of the bugles and the cry of the hunting dogs. Day and night the wild hunt was going on in the forests and gaps, persued the deer and destroyed the seeds. One day the King appeared on a clearing with his followers where a flock was put out to graze.

The shepherd was sitting before a hut, holding her sleeping child in her arms and next to her lay the shepherd dog. At once, the King's male dogs rushed at him and at the same time threw the woman paralyzed with fear to the ground. King Waze came and laughed. When the shepherd who had come running attacked the howling crowd, the King mad with anger set slaves and hundreds of men on the shepherd who was like his wife and child torn by the hounds in the end. Then a dull roaring arose and his own hounds choked the life out of him and his family. Their corpses turned into cold marble rocks'.

Vor langen Zeiten lebte im Berchtesgadener Land König Watze mit seiner Familie. Wegen seiner Grausamkeit beim Volke gefürchtet, erreichte ihn Gottes Zorn und er wurde mit seiner Frau und sieben Kindern zu starrem, kaltem Gestein verwandelt. Seit dieser Zeit ragt er nun als mächtiger Berg über das Land.

That's what the legend leaving the Watzmann in today's form with his wife and his children tells us. The mountain called Watzmann is an enormous massif with a number of independent tops and magnificent rock faces. Like the Matterhorn above Zermatt the Watzmann has with his wife and children become the landmark of Berchtesgaden. Its harmonious proportions and the Grünstein in front underline its characteristic dominant position. To the East of its feet we find Lake Königssee with the highest precipice of the Eastern Alps, the Watzmann-Ostwand, to the West the Wimbachtal filled with debris. Hocheck, Mittelspitze and Südspitze, once called Schönfeldspitze, are the names of the three tops of the main mountain crest.

Some 540 yards deeper a rigde passes the Watzmann children, leading further to the Watzmannfrau, also called 'Little Watzmann'.

It is no wonder that this legendary mountain attracted many people very soon when other investigations were still considered to be a necessary evil. Already at the beginning of the 18th century several crosses were mounted on the 8579-feet-high Hocheck and many believers went to this top on a pilgrimage.

But also scientists and clerics were interested in the highest elevation in the Berchtesgaden area. Valentin Stanig, a priest from Salzburg climbed the Hocheck during the surveyings in 1799 and wanted to continue his way to the obviously higher Mittelspitze.

He writes:
'I decided to climb this top that no human foot had walked on before. Loaded with my measuring instruments I set out for it. Already at the start I was angry, because I had to slide down a steep rock at the end of which a small ledge kept me from falling down to endless depth. Then I stepped over a dangerous place, one crevice beyond another. I thought better things have to come, but it was only worse. Soon I had to move on

crawling on a sharp mountain ridge and then again floating in the air in steep rock faces.

Often I needed to have an almost superhuman courage to not be overwhelmed by fearfulness, for most of the times I had to crawl over the sharp ridge that was surrounded by thousands of dangers at both sides. The single place one's must have the soul concentrated in it. Not even the most pious thought is allowed, but every step, every finger has strictly to be directed.

After I had come across a stable place again the mountain was very steep and with the greatest efforts I succeeded in reaching the highest elevation of the Watzmann. The people I left behind discovered me on this top piercing through the clouds with astonishment, joy and fear. The room up there on the top is so narrow that I could not compare it with any other mountain that I climbed...

Stanig's performance is still admirable, for this crossing would today have to be classified here and there with

Top: View from the 'Mittelspitze', the Watzmann's highest top with 8900 feet, across the ridge to the 'Südspitze'. You can easily discover the 'Biwakschachtel' (bivouac box) in the upper part of the Watzmann-Ostwand – marked by a circle. In the background on the left side of the 'Südspitze' the 'Hohen Tauern' with the 'Glocknergruppe' and the 'Kitzsteinhorn', and the Großvenediger on the right side.

the level of difficulty II (of medium difficulty) without the stairs carved out in the meantime and the ropes put up for the climbers' security.

This rope facilitating the crossing of the Watzmann (from the Hocheck across the Mittelspitze to the Südspitze) was put up in 1898 and renewed in 1979. Some 654 yards of rope were used and some 100 pitons were driven into the rock as the old ones had been severely damaged by lightning, freezing and thawing and represented a great security risk for the large number of climbers. Nevertheless, crossing the Watzmann rigde and the way down to the 'Wimbachtal' means an alpine adventure that should not be underestimated.

Another brilliant performance on this mountain was Johann Grill's climbing of the Eastern rock face of the Watzmann. After his alpine farm in the Ramsau Johann Grill was called the 'Kederbacher'. On the 6th June 1881 he lead Otto Schlück from Vienna within 14 hours through the 6233-feet-high 'Bartholomäwand', as this rock face was called at that time. Crossing this enormous rock face is still one of the great adventures in the Eastern Alps, in spite of the fact that it is frequented by 400 to 500 climbers a year. It is not so much its difficulty, but its structure and height that make up the special event. The ones who only want to climb will probably not be satisfied. Alone the climber who is good in finding paths, has a firm step, is expert, and knows about weather and snow conditions will be up to this rock face. From 1890 until today this rock face cost the lives of some 90 persons.

Report of the alpine rescue service 1974:

On the 16th June 2 men from Heppenheim and Mannheim, 30-year and 39-year-old, wanted to walk up to the top on the Salzburg path (level of difficulty V). After a bivouac in the 'Schöllhornkar' they reached the first ledge. Just when they were trying to secure at a security hook, a wet snow avalanche flew over them and injured one of the two. Completely soaked they put up their second bivouac beneath an overhang of the first ledge and were swept out of their hiding place by the mass of water plunging down. Because of the unfavourable weather conditions no-one could hear their distress signals. Only when their friends reported them missing the search for them was begun. On the 19th June, when the upper part of the rock face was still covered with fog, a helicopter could finally start and the place of their bivouac was found. The two exhausted climbers could be pulled aboard by means of a cable winch.

At an altitude of 6331 feet we find the 'Watzmannhaus' which belongs to the Munich section of the Alpine Club. It was built in 1887/1888 in order to facilitate climbing the Watzmann on the normal path. Today the 'Münchener Haus' is one of the most frequented huts of the Alpine Club in the Berchtesgaden mountains.

The 'bivouac box' put in 1951 beneath the 'Massiger Pfeiler' (massive pillar) in the Watzmann's Eastern rock face. It offers some security for several climbers in case of emergency and change of weather.

Südliches Gebirgspanorama von der Kneifelspitze

Jenner bis Reiteralpe

Southern mountain panorama from Kneifelspitze

Jenner to Reiteralpe

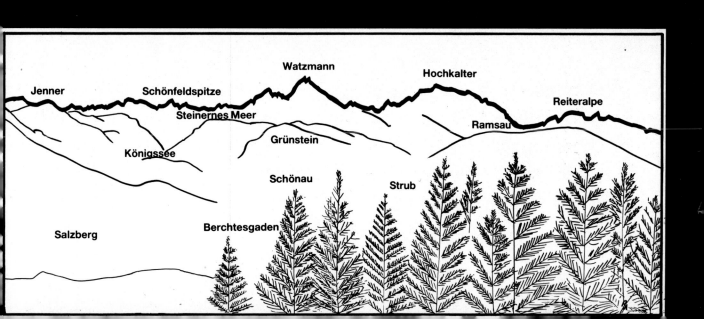

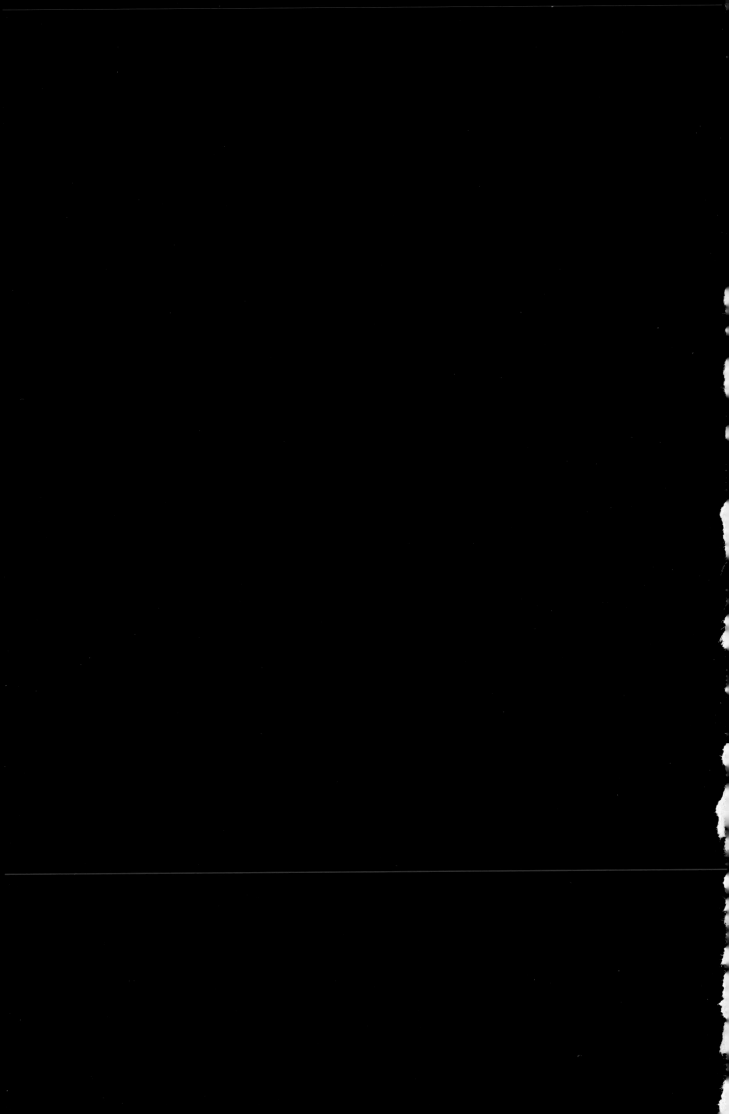

The Jenner

It is one of the most popular view points in the Berchtesgaden area and at same time an ideal setting-off point for mountain tours to the 'Hagengebirge'. This mountain is the only one in the valley basin that is disclosed by means of a cable railway. This railway, the cars of which are fastened to the suspension cable, surmounts a difference in altitude of 3936 feet at the lenght of 10,892 feet

Bottom: From the 'Pfaffenkogeln' we see the pyramidal form of the Jenner. Beneath the top, the top station of the Jenner cable railway leading up from the village of Königssee and disclosing the ambitious ski area of the Jenner. In summer it is the setting-off point for hikings and mountain tours to the 'Hagengebirge'. What you cannot see on this picture is the chair-lift leading from the 'Mitterkaser-Alm' (right bottom) up to the top station.

within 20 minutes. A ride on this cable railway is especially fascinating as the cars glide only a few yards over the alpine meadows and leisurely the landscape can be watched.

The Bavarian parliament permitted the construction of this cable railway under the condition that no other mountain railway project would follow in the former national park. This condition has been observed, except for the discussion about a cable railway to the Watzmann and the Jenner's further disclosure by lifts at its Southern side. When in 1977/1978 the Alpine Park was introduced some people wanted to separate this area from the centre of the Alpine Park and connect it with the Northern side of the Jenner that has already been disclosed by the cable railway and lifts. The attraction of the mountain for skiers should be increased, but for hikers and climbers it would have been without any consequences.

Left page, top: The top station of the Jenner cable railway after its opening. The paths to be seen in the background lead to the 'Schneibsteinhaus' and the 'Stahlhaus'.

Left page, centre: The 'Schneibstein-haus' at the 'Torrenerjoch' that can be reached from the Jenner within 40 minutes and is open the whole year through.

Left page, bottom: View from the 'Hohes Brett' down to the 'Torrener-joch' with the two huts, the 'Stahlhaus' in front and the 'Schneibsteinhaus' behind it. From here the 'Schneibstein', softly climbing up to the left, is one of the easiest mountains of about 6500 feet in the Berchtesgaden area that can be climbed within two hours. The winding paths on the left already belong to Austria and lead down to the 'Bluntautal'.

An easy path leads from the 5912-feet-high top station up to the 236-feet-higher top where a marvellous view to Lake Königssee, the 'Hagengebirge' and the 'Hohes Brett' is offered. Skiers wedel down on well-cared for, but ambitious pists to the village of Königssee, pists where in 1992 the olympic alpine competitions of men shall take place. But only if the International Olympic Committee comes to the decision that the Games shall be carried out in Berchtesgaden, respectively in the area of Southeastern Bavaria.

Perhaps you can watch the hang gliders on the Jenner who have their takeoff point beneath the top station since 1977. The hang glides' steering is done by weighting with the steering stirrup. Pushing this stirrup leads to an enlargement of the angle of incidence, pushing it to its reduction. In accordance, the glide's speed is reduced or inrcreased. A turn is done by pushing the stirrup to the left or to the right. In action, however, one needs to have much feeling and experience to find out the right proportioning for the desired direction and to always be flexible enough to manouver the glide safely considering the always existing troublemaking conditions like moving air and turbulences. Being one of the difficult mountains for hang gliding, the Jenner will for these reasons always be preserved to a small number of pilots who can see the wonderful Berchtesgaden area from the air.

Bottom: The snow-covered Jenner above the middle station of the Jenner. The chairs of the cable railway were replaced by cable cars in 1983 which means a great advantage when the weather is bad or when winter has come.

Top: Hang gliders, having started from the Jenner's top station, in front of the 'Hohes Brett'.

The Hagengebirge

A good half an hour away from the top station of the Jenner we find two huts, the 'Schneibsteinhaus' and the 'Carl-von-Stahl-Haus'. From the top of the 'Schneibstein' that can be reached within one and a half hours, we have an overwhelming view to the karstic plateau of the 'Hagengebirge'.

The two huts are also the setting-off point for two alpine ski tours, namely the so-called 'Kleine Reibe' (little tour) which leads to the 'Schneibstein', passes 'Lake Seeleinsee' and the 'Hohe Roßfelder' and offers a marvellous glissade, an ideal tour for one day.

The other ski tour is the 'Große Reibe' (big tour) for which at least two or three days have to be planned. Starting from the 'Schneibstein' as well, it leads almost endlessly across the 'Hagengebirge' to the Northern precipices of

Top: Starting from the top of the 'Schneibstein' and skiing down the 'Kleine Reibe', a ski tour coming down to 'Lake Seeleinsee' in a slight swing to the right.

Right page, top: 'Lake Seeleinsee' beneath the 'Hochseeleinseekopf' is a popular resting place of the ski tour called 'Kleine Reibe'.

Right page, bottom: Even the narrowest clefts of the rocks in the Alps are 'conquered' by special plants that have adapted to the extreme habitat. Leaf rosettes and low growth serve to reduce the evaporation and protect the plants against too low temperatures in winter those plants are almost immediately exposed to as they are often not covered by a protecting blanket of snow. Bryophytes belong to the most frequent plants of this interesting family of plants.

the 'Steinernes Meer' and up and down to the 'Kärlinger-haus' at the 'Funtensee'. The path goes on leading to the 'Ingolstädter Haus', the 'Hochwieskessel', the 'See-horn' and across the steep precipice of the 'Loferer Sei-lergraben' down to the 'Wimbachtal'. All in all this tour has the lenght of some 25 miles and some 8500 feet have to be climbed in several ascents.

We want to have a closer geological view to this marvel-lous karstic area. The history of the alpine landscape's evolution can be divided in three phases:

1. The rocks were mostly in oceans formed out of sedi-ments, out of shells and corals. This process of development took place some 220 million years ago and lasted for more than 100 million years.

2. Displacements of the earth's crust followed result-ing in the formation of the mountains and tensions resulted in their deformation. The process lasted again for about 100 million years.

3. Today's alpine landscape is formed by the earth crust's folding up and the erosion at the same time. This rise of the rocks and the creation of the valleys lasted for 10 million years and in some places of the mountains it has not yet been terminated. The earth-quakes in the Southern Alps every now and then are a proof for that.

A climatic event during the last millions of years has especially determined the landscape: the Ice Age. On the plateaus and cirques huge masses of wet snow were formed from which enormous glacial streams reached into the foreland. The 'Steinernes Meer' and the 'Hagen-

Top: An interesting view of the 'Hagengebirge' from the 'Hundstod' in the 'Steinernes Meer'. On the very left side we seen the 'Schneibstein', in the centre of the picture the 'Kahlersberg', the two 'Teufelshörner' on the right side and the glacial 'Dachstein' at the horizon.

gebirge' were the setting-off point of the enormous Königssee-glacier whose icemasses excavated the bottom of Lake Königssee nearly 380 yards below the bottom of the valley.

The limestone's special quality to dissolve in acid waters, a process called karstification is added, an occurrence the Berchtesgaden Alps are especially involved in as the extensive plateaus offer ideal condi-tions for the water's attack. The karstic rocks in the 'Steinernes Meer' and the 'Hagengebirge' are good examples for that.

We can immediately witness and observe these geolo-gical processes. Whether it is the silent trickling away of the water in spring or the immense thunder of a rock-fall, it is always a piece of a mountain that is taken apart and the area's face that is being changed slowly and in a hardly perceptible way.

The 'Röth' – the 'Steinernes Meer'

In a large bend the plateau of the 'Hagengebirge' South of Lake Königssee is combined with the 'Steinernes Meer'. The connection is called the 'Röth', far away with a number of chamois and ibex. In former times it was like many other places used as meadow land.

Bottom: Observing a rock goat in the remote area of the 'Röth' South of Lake Königssee in the centre of the national park.

'Don't forget one element of the traffic: two legs and two feet. A chair-lift does not have to be built up on every view mountain where a bar would come up as well. Hiking to the beautiful and lonely places belongs to the traffic, too (Theodor Heuss, Federal President of Germany, during his opening speech of the German traffic exhibition in Munich, 1953).

Already in the 9th century there were alpine pastures in the Berchtesgaden area. They came up because of the necessity to keep as many cows as possible. So the alpine farmers found themselves compelled to create additional pastures for their cattle. The cows were lead to the alpine pastures in May and came back to the valley in October. The hay made during this time on the alpine pastures serves to feed the animals in winter; the animals' grazing in the valley pastures was only necessary when they were down in the valley.

A three-step process of working, the regular change from one alpine pasture to the other has developed in the Berchtesgaden area. As the vegetation's evolution is delayed the higher you go, a three-step use of the pastures is necessary. As most of the alpine pastures were to be found at an altitude of 2000 to 6000 feet the alpine farmers had the chance to come down from a higher pasture if they were surprised by possible snow falls in summer.

Example for the three-step work on alpine farms: the 'Saletalm' at the most distant corner of Lake Königssee was the lowest pasture, the pastures belonging to it were the 'Funtenseealm' at 'Lake Funtensee' and – higher again – the 'Feldalm' at the 'Feldkogel' in the 'Funtensee area'.

The most distant alpine pastures, those at the edge of the 'Steinernes Meer', could only be reached after several days' marches and nightly rests on particular pastures. Often the farmer had to master positively dangerous passages with his cattle. A great advantage for this was the breed of cows of that time. The cows were called the 'Berchtesgaden cats', were very small and light, but in return agile and secure to step on even the narrow mountain paths. Many of the paths used by climbers today were the cattle paths in former times.

Since the middle of the 19th century an increasing decline of the alpine farms is remarkable. After a very low point around the 1970s an improvement, not least because of governmental premiums, has been able to be observed. So the number of the alpine pastures amounts to 23 in the area of the national park, whereas in 1837 it was 90.

The alpine huts in the Berchtesgaden area deserve a special look. After the Latin word 'casa' they are called 'Kaser'. These huts, round buildings without any windows, were at first enlarged by a stable around the whole hut. The fact that the living space is completely protected against the wind by the stable and is warmed up by it as well is of great advantage. This type of hut is unique to the Berchtesgaden area and cannot be found anywhere else in the Alps.

Top: View from top of the 'Hochkalter' to the most remote part of the 'Wimbachtal'. The 'Watzmann-Südspitze' at the left top, the area of the 'Steinernes Meer', a karstic plateau, on the right side.

Right page, top: The former alpine pastures around Lake Funtensee at the height of 5249 feet in the 'Steinernes Meer', in the background we see the 'Schottmalhorn'. Up to the 1960s these alpine pastures were still used, but unfortunately the huts dilapidated more and more during the following years.

Right page, bottom: The less inclined hills in the 'Funtensee' area are covered by plants like alpine roses etc., plants that easily grow between rock and more or less deep soil.

The Hochkalter

The mountain of 'Hochkalter', lying West of the Watzmann is one of the most beautiful mountains in the Berchtesgaden area. It is more isolated with its Southern parts being rather secluded. Because of its alpine difficulties it is reserved to expert climbers only. The top is only 147 feet lower than that of the Watzmann. The huge wooded area on the Northern and Western side seems to isolate the top and gives it the impression of being a self-contained mountain, removed from life in the valleys beneath.

Where the German Alpine Road enters the Ramsau valley at the pass 'Schwarzbachwacht' between the 'Lattengebirge' and the 'Reiteralpe' a view is offered to the Northern side of the 'Hochkalter'. Here we discover the 'Blaueis' that is normally hidden from our eyes by the mountain. The 'Blaueis' is the northernmost glacier of the Alps. It is by no means a large glacier, it lacks the wet snow reserves of the Central or Western Alps and it has been strongly marked by the glacial formation's decline. Nevertheless, it is a real glacier with clefts and a crevice at the edge. It is a steep glacier, with inclinations of 55 degrees filling the 'Hochkar' with its length of 0.6 mile and its width of 475 yards between the 'Hochkalter' and the 'Blaueisspitze'. In spring it is an alpine icy-cold ski slope.

The mountains following South of the 'Hochkalter' belong to loneliness: 'Ofental', 'Ofentalhörndl', 'Steintal', 'Steintalhörndl', 'Sittersbachtal'. These valleys that are parallel to the Northern side of the 'Hochkalter' and the ridges lying in between, are the places for experts familiar with the locality trying to escape from crowds of people on much-frequented tops in summer and worn-out pists in winter. Above its wooden zone there are no laid out and secured paths any more.

Further to the South we find the 'Hocheisspitze', the highest top of a group of summits surrounding the debris-filled 'Hocheiskar' in the form of a horse shoe. The ridge leading West across the 'Hochkammerlinghorn', the 'Kammerlinghorn' and the 'Karlkogel' to the pass of the 'Hirschbichl' and leading South and Southwest across the 'Alpelhorn', the 'Sigeretkopf', the 'Wimbachscharte' and the 'Kühleitenschneid' connecting it with the 'Hundstod' and the 'Steinernes Meer', signifies the border between Bavaria and Austria. The two boldly ragged 'Palfenhörner' towering above these huge masses of debris form the end of the 'Wimbachtal' still belonging to the 'Hochkalter' and the Southern 'Wimbachtal'.

Nowhere within a wide radius we can observe the decay of the mountains, their dissolution to dreary screes as well as in the Southern 'Wimbachtal'. There is no bright and firm Dachstein limestone like on the 'Hoher Göll' for example, alone the crumbly Ramsau dolomite is its building stone. It is drizzling and crumbling everywhere, the ridges are furrowed and the rock faces are ragged and huge masses of debris form around the base of the mountains. Step by step the decay is going on, wind and waters, the frost with its explosive effect and the destroying power of the avalanches are the silently working forces.

Already in 1893 Ludwig Purtscheller, a well-known explorer of the Alps, considered the 'Hochkalter' to be 'the summit similar to a half-dilapidated castle'. These were prophetic words, for already on the 24th August 1908 this castle crashed because of a rock-slide. An eyewitness who watched the rock-slide from the opposite 'Watzmann-Hocheck' reports: 'Suddenly I heard such an ear-splitting noise that I had to turn my head to the West. I could not help thinking that the 'Hochkalter' had exploded. At once I saw a huge grey-black cloud raising with an incredible pandemonium from the summit like from a volcano becoming wider and more immense and soon surrounding the whole mountain with a sinister smoke and darkening the sun...'.

In February 1959, a rock face of the height of 492 feet and the width of 230 feet between the two 'Palfenhörner' broke. Like a stream of lava several thousands of cubic yards of rock poured over the 'Wimbachtal' covered with a blanket of wet snow and at last divided in three branches of 1600, 980 and 650 feet. Rocks of the size of rooms towered at either side of the stream, leaving yards-high snow walls as well. The snow warmed up by the immense compression and friction stiffened to become glass-like and hard ice.

Miraculously, no human being was injured in these environmental catastrophes on the 'Hochkalter'.

Top: View across Lake Hintersee to the 'Hochkalter'. In the middle we see the snow-covered glacier 'Blaueisgletscher', the northernmost glacier in the Alps. Left of it the pointed 'Schärtenspitze'. Further to the right the 'Blaueisspitze' and the top of the 'Hochkalter' as the highest elevation.

Bottom: The stalk-less Enzian and Silberwurz, both being protected.

The neighbouring communities

Ramsau

At one side of the road, documented already in 1386, connecting the convent of Salzburg across the 'Hirschbichl' with its possessions in the 'Pinzgau' the village of Ramsau was erected. The houses were built up along the road on the valley's bottom. On both sides of the road alpine farms developed on the moraine terraces climbing up to the height of 3280 feet and expanding over to the 'Taubensee'.

Ramsau is completely bound up with its alpine mountains, the Watzmann and the Hochkalter look right into the windows of the farmers. One side of the valley is limited by the Hoher Göll, the opposite side by the Reiteralpe. To the North steep meadows become wooded rounded mountain tops offering a good view. Pastures and many mountain forests surround the area. It is not without a good reason that Saint Vinzenz, the woodcutters' patron saint figures in Ramsau's emblem.

The old way from Berchtesgaden to Ramsau avoided the glen of the brook, only the modern technique of road construction made it possible to build the road between rocky spurs and roaring waters. Another entry leads from the 'Saalachtal' across the pass 'Schwarzbachwacht' into the village of Ramsau. This way has been used very often and today it is part of the German Alpine Road's route. The old road across the 'Hirschbichl' is preserved for pedestrians, it has been closed off to the traffic. Lately a road from Bischofswiesen leading across the 'Hochschwarzeck' has been finished.

Glens and passes, these are the reasons why Ramsau could preserve its originality, even though the settlement became bigger and bigger, forming a real community centre around the church. Ramsau covers a large area: the 'Roßhofschmiede' behind Ilsank, the 'Schwarzeck', the pass of 'Schwarzbachwacht', the lake of Hintersee, the Wonderwood, fountains of glaciers, the 'Wimbachklamm', Wimbachtal, the Soleleitungsweg, Hirschbichl, Taubensee, Mordau can be found here. The winter's attraction is the feeding of game in Ramsau. The 'Kunterweg' chapel is an old peasant pilgrimage church and the population of Ramsau still celebrates old peasant holidays, rural processions and has preserved a very old dialect with rural timbre, their old traditional costumes and their traditions.

Here the change of one season to the other becomes very evident. The contrast between flourishing meadows and glancing wet snow in spring, the green landscape in summer, the colourful autumn and the white winter is marvellous and new worlds are created. But nobody can tell during what season Ramsau looks most beautiful and is most attractive.

The world-known view of the Ramsau church with the 'Reiteralpe' in the background. The outstanding 'gugelhupf' in the middle of the picture is the 'Wagendrischlhorn' with 7,385 feet. In front of the church we see the old, walled-in graveyard where we can find the grave of Ramsau's best-known son, the mountain guide 'Kederbacher', Johann Grill. An interesting fact that deserves being mentioned is that in the 19th century all pictures of the Ramsau church showed the church in the opposite direction, with the 'Hoher Göll' in the background.

The Ramsau mountain guide Johann Grill, called the 'Kederbacher' (1835-1917).

Der Kederbacher um 1885

Johann Grill, after his mountain farm called the 'Kederbacher', was the first man to climb the Watzmann's Eastern rock face. He was the best-known man of Ramsau. In 1917, in the middle of World War I, the English Alpine Club's president, Farrar, wrote about him:

'... I speak my mind that he was one of the greatest mountain climbers of his time, that there was not half a dozen of mountain guides in the entire area of the Alps when his great time had come in the 1870s and at the beginning of the 1880s who could be compared to him and none who would have been head and shoulders above him.

Considering the fact that he was 45 before he had the opportunity to show what he was one can only suppose with admiration to what culmination his anyway great climbing career would have risen. And that after having spent his life in a small mountain valley whose

mountains are not higher than 9000 feet. He was born the 22nd October 1835 and during his youth he seemingly had hardly the chance to make himself a name as mountain guide as the summer holiday makers who would visit Berchtesgaden at that time did not have any ambition in that direction. In opposition to that he distinguished himself as a driver on courtly hunts by his unsurpassable climbing in an area of limestone mountains where great climbing qualities are necessary...'

In 1868 Kederbacher together with his neighbour Punz succeeded in crossing the three summits of the Watzmann and the difficult 'Hochkammerlinghorn'. His reputation was already high when he succeeded in the first ascent of the 'Tribulaun' in the Stubai valley where Swiss mountain guides had failed. Farrar continues to write:

'... In the same way he completed the first ascent to the 'Königsspitze' starting from the 'Suldenjoch', a long difficult climbing with many stairs to be hewed out. One has to mention that in his home there is only one minor glacier, the 'Blaueisgletscher'... In May 1881 he underlined his reputation as an excellent pathfinder by leading Otto Schlück through the Watzmann's enormous Eastern rock face. At that time this was one of the greatest problems in the Eastern Alps and still today crossing it is very difficult. That can be realized by the fact that no less than 26 men of the 34 who repeated this ascent by 1909 found themselves compelled to bivouac. The vertical height of this rock face is 5905 feet (whereas the 'Matterhorn' towers up 3959 feet above the 'Schweizer Hütte'!). The whole rock face has an incline to the large, is very complicated making it difficult to find one's way and demanding permanent strong and often rather difficult climbing...'

So far Farrar about the best-known son of Ramsau.

Left: Johann Grill, called the 'Kederbacher' at the age of some 30 years. On the 6th June 1881 he crossed the Watzmann's Eastern rock face as a mountain guide for the first time. Beyond any doubt Kederbacher was the best-known German mountain guide of his time. He was acknowledged by the guides of the Western Alps at that time as well and astonishingly often the travelled to the mountains in Switzerland and France.

Right page: In votive pictures one can see the close connection between piety, tradition, theology and folk art. The opposite votive picture to be seen in the pilgrimage church Our Dear Lady in 'Kunterweg' above Ramsau tells about the owner of the upper 'Rehlegg' fief who had come to the greatest misery through his own illness, the infirmity of his wife and also the epidemics of his animals. For the relief of his misery he solemnly vowed to the Queen of grace to have a book printed about the aim and object of going on a pilgrimage. His request was granted, he met his vow and had in addition this interesting votive picture painted.

Año. 1750. hat dise Tafl anhero geopfert. Joseph Rihlögger sambt seinen Zwey eheweibern, vnd khindtern, Vnd wegen einen Vieckfall, Gott vnd Maria auf den Condtersvieg, vnd denen H. Zwey fürbiter S. Leonhartus vnd Ignätj. Zü schuldiger Danckhbartheit Zü vermehren

This picture was sacrificed here by Joseph Rihlögger and his two wives and children and is to add to his grate-fulness towards the Lord, the Queen of grace Maria and the two Saints Leonhartus and Ignätj.

Bischofswiesen

This community, the second largest in Bavaria, deduces its name from 'Wiese des Bischofs' (pasture of the bishop). It refers to a Salzburg bishop who in 1155 exchanged this area against a farm in Lower Austria. This exchange and the name that was given at that time found its painted expression in the community's emblem showing a so-called 'Feldkasten' (case in the fields) on a green meadow and two crossed episcopal staffs in blue behind it.

As its points of interest we should mention the frontier fortifications around the pass of 'Hallthurm' from the 12th century, the pilgrimage church in 'Loipl' and the marvellous view of the mountains on the 'Kastensteiner-wand'.

The mountain chain of the 'Lattengebirge' closing the area to the West and consisting of the 'Karkopf' and the 'Rotofentürme' towering above the pass of 'Hallthurm' is interesting for us. In common parlance the latter are called 'Montgelas-Nase' (nose of Montgelas) after Duke Max von Montgelas, a controverse minister under the regency of King Louis I (1768-1868). The Chronicles tell: '... on the 'Lattengebirge'... the peculiar 'Montgelas-Nase'... this funny mountain chain with the traits of an old woman reminding King Louis so lively of his minister that he immortalized his name in the mountain...

Not far away from the 'Rotofentürme' we find the 'Steinerne Agnes' (stony Agnes), a 32 feet high top that demands excellent climbing. The legend of the 'stony alpine dairy maid' winds around this strange rocky figure. One version goes like that: The alpine dairy maid Agnes was known to be the most beautiful girl in all of the valley. That filled her with immoderate pride so that she refused

all the men courting her until she met a dashing young hunter who broke her heart. He seduced her and she awaited her child's birth. The hunter left her. Then the devil took possession of her and in her despair and fear of the scorn and derision of her girl-friends she killed the newborn baby on a lonely path through the forests above the 'Rotofenalm'. A clap of thunder was to be heard and she was turned into a huge stone looking down from the precipitous rock like a warning.

Unequalled in beauty is the 'Maximilians-Reitweg', a path leading from the 'Aschauerweiherbad' (swampy swimming pool) to the pass of 'Hallthurm' along the brooks and past centuries-old mountain maples, a path that is unequalled in its category.

The 'meadows of the bishop' were during the past years enormously built up and spoilt. One can only hope that the politically responsible persons can struggle through to preserve further endangered parts of the community to the natives and tourists in their originality.

Left page, bottom: View from the 'Lattengebirge' to the valley of Bischofswiesen with the section 'Winkl' in front, behind it we see Bischofswiesen and the small ledge of the view point of the 'Kastensteinerwand'. Above that all, the impressive massif of the 'Hoher Göll'.

This page, top: The 'Sleeping Witch' and the 'Montgelas-Nase' can easily be seen from Loipl.

This page, bottom: Hut belonging to the Grublehen (fief) built in blocks in the 18th century, above the 'Umgehungsbrücke', a picture from patriarchal times.

65

Maria Gern

If you look from Berchtesgaden, a narrow valley leads up towards the 'Untersberg'. Here and there we see green meadows, the whitewashed walls of a farm and in the middle of the cleft the onion dome of Maria Gern. In the old days it was only called Gern, later on it became an independent community and today it belongs to the community of Berchtesgaden. Already in the 17th century Gern was a popular and well-known place of pilgrimage with the church covering a picture of the Virgin Mary, hence the name Maria Gern.

Maria Gern is mainly a farming community, only in the latest past several country houses have been built there. Some farms cling to the steep meadows, those farms at the higher altitudes border the face of the 'Untersberg'. The fiefs of Klapflehen and Bischoflehen offer marvellous view points. The church, the guesthouse, the sexton's house and the former school make up a picturesque group, the church showing a special style and charm. It was built in rural, bright rococo and its altars, ornaments and its wrought-iron gratings belong to the rococo as well. The two most beautiful views are offered from the church, one towards the 'Untersberg'

This page, top: Light procession the evening before the patron saint's anniversary in the church of Maria Gern taking place on the second golden sunday. Seeing the illuminated windows of the houses and the members of the procession with their colourful candle lights in the early evening of the short days of October is especially impressive.

This page, bottom: The fief 'Fendtleitenlehen' opposite the pilgrimage church, a well-preserved farm. The stable house with two levels was built in 1685 (proved by the main girder in the house's dining room), but its base should be older. Impressive again the Watzmann with its characteristic figure.

Left page: The pilgrimage church of Maria Gern with the Southern precipices of the legendary 'Untersberg'. At the beginning of the 18 th century the church was built in rococo for the special worship of the Queen of graces; the first mass in this church was held in 1710.

with its enormous red Southern rock faces and towards the other side the Watzmann in the distance.

The development of the fiefs

In the preceding pages we have sometimes used the notion of 'fief' meaning a farm and this notion should be expained. The settlers, farmers and woodcutters coming from the 'Pinzgau' to Berchtesgaden in the 12th century formed fellowships the presidents of which were both heads of the community and beadles. They were the representatives towards the cleirical government in Berchtesgaden. The fellowships existed up to this century. The clearing, fertilization and cultivation of the land were carried out through team work. The farms having developed were lent to the subjects against a certain amount of payment.

From 1937 on these fiefs could be bought (fief = land owned by the local royalty). So the fiefs became the farmer's property, the farmers having to pay a rent fixed in the hereditary papers. The subjects themselves, however, remained villeins, but not in the sense of strict villeinage of that time. In Berchtesgaden it only determined that people could not marry without the permission of the convent and could not leave the country (wood workers especially).

The hereditary papers allowed the farmers to divide their properties into two or three parts. So many small fiefs came up because of this division that the owner often had to find a secondary occupation to feed himself and his family. If he was not a minor or a woodworker he worked on a wood-turning lathe or carved other woodware that became known in the world as Berchtesgadener Ware.

The 'Theresienklause' at the upper end of the glen was a water barrage built by the royal saltworks administration in 1834/35. The dammed up water served for log drifting, some 1000 cubic metres of stacked wood being floated down to the wire-screen near the 'Untersberg' marble grinding mill. Log drifting is the transportation on water of loose logs. For this purpose water was dammed up and the dry bed of the brook in front of the barrage was filled with logs. After the floodgates being opened the highly compressed water swept the wood through the narrow glen with logs wedged at narrower places having to be put back into the current by means of long sticks of the woodworkers. For stopping the logs a wire-screen was built at the end of the glen. As long as both saltworks in Berchtesgaden were run by the energy of burnt wood, log-shifting was great in demand; shifting through the 'Almbachklamm' served to supply the saltworks of Schellenberg which was closed already in 1805.

This page, top and bottom: An interesting and eventful path leads through the 'Almbachklamm', laid out by pathfinders from Ingolstadt in 1894. 29 bridges and footbridges had to be built for its practicability, 320 stony stairs and a little tunnel were dynamited out of the rocks.

Ettenberg

On a lookout point between Maria Gern and the pass above the valley of Schellenberg we find the village of Ettenberg. A steep road from Marktschellenberg leads up to this old place of pilgrimage that can be reached by foot as well from Maria Gern through the 'Almbachklamm' on a wonderful walk. The picture of Mary's visitation is venerated in the church that was built by Prince Bishop Juilius Heinrich von Rehlingen in 1724/25. In the old days the church was full of votive pictures asking the heavenly powers for helping the pilgrims.

Those pictures going back to the end of the 17th century are interesting because of the colourful variety of the represented events.

Quite interesting is a votive picrure pointing to the dangers the cows are exposed to on alpine pastures. It indicates the degree of truth of tales reporting that the cattle can be injured by the bites of poisonous snakes.

On the mentioned picture a man and a woman kneel in the middle of steep mountains on a meadow. In front of them we see a cushion with four infants on, besides a billygoat, a sheep, a cow and in the middle of the picture we see snakes, toads, salamanders, all oversized compared with the surroundings.

Obviously, the fear of these sinister animals has lead to the unnatural enlargement on the picture.

Top: Wonderul building at the foot of the 'Untersberg', the church and a guesthouse next to it. The green meadow beneath the yellow walls belongs to the 'Scheibenkaser', a former alpine pasture.

Bottom: The interior of the lately renovated church in Ettenberg, once called 'Almberg'.

Marktschellenberg

This village is situated right between Berchtesgaden and Salzburg. We find the village of Ettenberg and the 'Almbachklamm' on the side of the 'Untersberg' and Scheffau and the 'Mehlweg' (path) on the other.

Schellenberg was the gate to Salzburg, after Berchtesgaden the largest settlement of the former episcopal area. The settlement came up in the narrow, often dangerous valley of the brook, after salt had been found in the 12th century near Dürrnberg and Goldenbach. Its saltwater was pumped through wooden pipes to be boilt in a boiler near Schellenberg.

Already in the 13th century the village developed at both sides of the brook, but the eventful up and down in history, the pawnage to Salzburg and the impoverishment caused life in misery and drudgery to the people of Schellenberg. The saltworks was closed already in 1805 and torn down 100 years later. Some redevelopment was tried, but only tourism of our century has helped to make Schellenberg a flourishing village.

When Martin Luther's teachings arrived in the clerical princedoms of Berchtesgaden and Salzburg, they were accepted very well especially in Scheffau and Oberau, as Saxon and Berchtesgaden miners were employed in the salt mine of Dürrnberg and were very fond of the new interpretation. For the farmers it was good news, too, promising above all an improvent of their economic situation.

The counteractions of the clerical authorities culminated 200 years later, during the first third of the 18th century, in the protestants' expulsion and emigration some thousands settling in Saxony and the area around Nuremberg. Their particular industry brought them to considerable wealth. So nobody can tell whether the rise of the Nuremberg toy industry is closely connected with the settling of the Berchtesgaden emigrants, as all Berchtesgadeners were familiar with toys as well.

An interesting point is the marble grinding mill at the end of the 'Almbachklamm'. Stefan Pfnür, the owner of the near-by guesthouse and miller by profession, is the last one to run a marble grinding mill, but more or less only for the attraction of the guests of his restaurant. The tourists keep the mill alive by buying souvenirs there. According to several documents the mill's products, marble balls, were transported to Francfort and Nuremberg already in the 16th century to finally be shipped on sailing boats from Hamburg, Rotterdam, Amsterdam and London to East- and West India. The old documents reveal that these marble balls, packed in bags and casks were a welcome ballast for the sailing boats.

The principle of the marble grinding mill is the following: Through a small canal water is directed to several water grooves, the streaming water drives a horizontal waterwheel. This waterwheel is the upper part of the veritable grinder consisting of two sandstone disks where the cube-shaped marble pieces are ground to round marble balls of different sizes in the grindstone's grooves made in advance. The grindstone's base is fixed whereas according to the water flowing to the waterwheel turns and grinds.

Top: The miles-long South-East precipice of the 'Untersberg' and the valley of Schellenberg in front.

Centre, bottom: Extraordimary ice figures in the 'Schellenberger Eishöhle' which in 1925 was disclosed by stairs and banisters. The astonished eyes of the visitors discover here shafts, halls and domes made of the icy-shining underground of the 'Untersberg'.

Right page, bottom: The 'Stöhrhaus', a hut of the Berchtesgaden section of the Alpine Club, beneath the summit of the 'Berchtesgadener Hochthron', the setting-off point for extreme climbings in the Southern rock faces of the 'Untersberg'.

The 'Untersberg' towers up miles-long North of the valley of Schellenberg with steep precipices and jagged rock faces. Besides the Watzmann the Untersberg is one of the most popular and most frequented mountains in Berchtesgaden. It can easily be climbed and offers a marvellous view when visibility is good. A tour on the cable car from the Austrian village of St. Leonhard and the following crossing of the jagged plateau to the 'Berchtesgadener Hochthron', the highest elevation of this massive mountain 6469 feet, is especially popular.

It is known that this mountain is steeped in legends. The best-known legend is that of the Emperor Charles in the interior of the 'Untersberg':

At the time of the heathens a wild tribe of dwarfs had excaveted the Untersberg. Its halls are big and tremendous. Green pastures expand down there, wonderful flowers grow here and rich fountains flow. Twelve entries lead outside to the Berchtesgaden area. The emperor Charles the Great is enthroned in a large hall whose ceilings glance with jewels. He is surrounded by dukes, the great and the army of his empire. He rests on a marble chair with a sparkling crown on his head and the sceptre in his right hand. His white beard, plaited with a precious string of pearls covers the golden breast of his clothes and twists twice around the table. From time to time the emperor awakes from his sleep. A page is subsequently sent to the 'Geiereck' to see if the ravens still circle around the mountain. If this is the case, the page brings the message and the emperor turns his head with a faint lamentation and falls back to his old stiffness.

But as soon as the beard of Charles the Great is wound around the table three times, his time will have come. Heading his army he will come out of the mountains, fight a bloody battle against the arch-enemies as Germany will be in a desperate misery. So much blood will flow that it will stream into the warrants' shoes. But the Emperor Charles the Great will successfully stand the fight and ride off after having won the battle on the back of his three-legged white horse'.

Left page, top: The marble grinding mill at the end of the 'Almbachklamm', the last marble grinding mill in Germany.

Left page, bottom: The valley of Schellenberg. The plain in the background is the Austrian 'Flachgau' around Salzburg.

Right page, top: Band in a procession in Marktschellenberg.

Right page, bottom: Kajakers on the Berchtesgaden brook shortly before Schellenberg. Here they have to get off because of a following dam.

Unterau and Oberau

In the valley of the Berchtesgaden brook we find Unterau at 1640 feet above sea level and at 3600 feet above sea level the village of Oberau. In between, there are farms, partly hidden like oases in the middle of green forests, partly open we discover houses in the meadow farms, guesthouses, the church, the school and the sawmill. The Oberau's situation in the sun is marvellous, the view that is offered is excellent, lovely low highlands in the reflection of the grand 'Untersberg' rock faces and the gigantic faces of the 'Hoher Göll' to the South-East.

The former sign of the community of Au, which due to the regional reform came to Berchtesgaden in 1972 showed crossed miners' mallet and hammer which is to be explained by the geographic and economic situation of the community. Situated between two salt mines, the mine of Berchtesgaden on one side and the mine of Dürrn-

Left page, bottom: At the summit of the Roßfeld road between the 'Roßfeld' and the 'Oberahornkaser'. The great road constructions in the Berchtesgaden area between the 'Reiteralpe' and the 'Roßfeld' for which some 50 million marks were invested in the time of the National Socialism in the 1930s are typical examples of mountain roads that were not built according to the road conditions, but in the intention to disclose the natural beauties of the alpine landscape to the owners of a motor vehicle.

The German Alpine Road starting at the Lake of Constance that was not finished due to World War II was to end in a grand bow the Berchtesgaden valley basin at an altitude of 5249 feet along the Bavarian-Austrian border.

After the war the absence of this stretch signified a regettable gap as this distance of 0.6 mile is the showpiece of a project that had swallowed up millions and in reality had only been begun because of this stretch. From the rigde one has a view down to Salzburg and the 'Dachstein' and to the 'Tennen-

berg where salt has been mined already in prehistoric times on the other people from Au found work as miners and still can find it today.

Finally parts of the Austrian salt deposits at Dürrnberg are situated in Au on Bavarian ground. This problem has been controled in 1829 by the so-called 'saltworks convention'.

In summertime Au is bright and rich in sunlight, offering many paths for walks and hikings, the Roßfeld road disclosing a wonderful elevated area. In winter, the wide, slightly inclined meadowed land, in combination with the area around Dürrnberg is a fine place for skiing. The alpine area with its good snow-conditions can easily be reached by cars and buses through the Roßfeld road and has been disclosed by innumerable lifts. Owing to the situation at the North side of the 'Roßfeld' skiing can be started here in late autumn and finishes no earlier than at the end of April. The whole year through Au offers itself to be a popular and attractive holiday resort.

gebirge' across the mountains of 'Salzkammergut' on one side and to the 'Untersberg' and the 'Reiteralpe' across the Berchtesgaden valley basin on the other. Close by the 'Hoher Göll' towers up above this stretch with its rock faces cut through by ledges and huge precipices at the Eastern and Northern sides.

For almost 15 years the building sites lay fallow and the project interrupted by the war was exposed to decay. In 1953 the construction of the road was continued the money spent having to be provided from a toll that is imposed to the users of that road. Now the most beautiful part of the German Alpine Road has been completed.

Right page, centre: For the 60th anniversary of the foundation of the society for the continued use of traditional costumes 'd'Weißenstoana' a tent was erected.

Right page, bottom: View of Oberau in summer.

Picture above: View of Schönau in front of the 'Grünstein' and the Watzmann. The 'Grünstein' in the foreground of the Watzmann offers an excellent view of all the Berchtesgaden area. It can be climbed within one and a half hours from Hammerstiel.
Beneath its summit the 'Grünsteinhütte' (hut of the Alpine Club) awaits the tired hiker with a good snack under cool trees.

Left page, bottom:
The centre of Schönau.

Right page, bottom: A panoramic view of Schönau towards the 'Hoher Göll', the 'Brett' and the 'Jenner'.

Schönau am Königssee

This community developed in the course of the regional reform in 1978 from the communities Schönau and Königssee.

Schönau has the form of a wide triangle, a plateau having come up from ice-aged side moraines. No other name but 'Schönau' (beautiful meadowland) could be more apt, for it is a landscape of meadows and parks going down on either side to the romantic valleys of the Ramsau brook on one side and the Königssee brook on the other. Nowhere can we find a central settlement, the houses are scattered over the area, dispersed, each of them standing alone, surrounded by gardens and trees among which we can also find old, magnificent mountain maples. A view is offered at all sides, one feels like standing on a revolving stage, the massif of the 'Hoher Göll' coming up from the Unterstein valley, the 'Untersberg' forming the picturesque background to the North,

the 'Lattengebirge' protects against wind and weather and the 'Reiteralpe' and the 'Hochkalter' are greatly to see. Only the 'Watzmann' is too close so that is does not have an effect. The Grünstein in front of it towers up immediately over the plateau. The settlement of fiefs was complemented by villas, guesthouses and country houses, even and easy walking paths through the length and the breadth of the area. Nevertheless, Schönau has remained an excellent restful residential district.

Königssee was never a village in the usual sense with church, inn and school, it has never been a closed settlement, but always a number of single houses, solitary settlements scattered over the area between the shore of Lake Königssee and the station of Berchtesgaden. Here again, we find the combination of old farms, guesthouses and inns.

From the Königssee there is not only a path to the beautiful 'Malerwinkel' and the possibility to take a ride on a boat across Lake Königssee, but also a cool path along the brook to Berchtesgaden, paths to the Schönau plateau and to Unterstein and also the Jenner cable railway from the top station of which there are again more possibilities for hikings and walks. In winter the 'Jenner' is as popular as it is in summer, additional lifts have made it an exceptional ski area. Another excellent construction, the toboggan run of artificial ice has confirmed Königssee's reputation as winter resort. National and world championships in tobogganing and bobsledding are held here. It is of advantage that this run can easily be reached and does not have too great a solar radiation. All that would be ideal preconditions for possible Olympic competitions in 1992.

Traditions

The spatial isolation of Berchtesgaden and its century-long political and clerical independence have lead to traditions that despite all influences from outside are preserved today and are in many aspects different from the traditions of the near surroundings. Their roots date back to times long past, essentially determined by the religion, the professional life, natural occurrences and the course of human life. The visitor of our area can still see many of the deeply-rooted traditions. But he will be offered folkloristic junk here as well as in probably all areas with much tourism. For the tourists it will be hard to draw the line between real tradition and mere show. In the following we will try to describe some of the traditions.

Right: Saluting gun, traditional hat with a 'Gamsbart' made of the hair of a chamois, hunting knife and 'Charivari'.

The salute guns of the members of the Berchtesgaden Christmas Rifle Clubs are pistols whose barrels made of iron or steel hardly surpasses the short, heavy shaft of nutwood. The capsules are put on one side of the shaft, the trigger is operated, a tension spring moves the gun's hammer and beats the detonator cap. The sparkle inflames the load of black powder put into the shaft and dammed by a wooden plug. Every riflemen has to have a wooden hammer or mallet on him to put in the wooden plug.

The traditional hat is not the hat of a Berchtesgaden rifleman, but a hat from the 'Chiemgau' which sometimes is worn here as well. The hat is also decorated by a 'Gamsbart' or a 'Hirschbart'. To avoid any error, the 'Bart' means the hair at the back of either a chamois or a stag that is torn out of the shot animals. The hair is sized, bound together by threads to small bunches, length and colour of the hair having to be observed. 30,000 to 40,000 hair are bound together by a 'Gamsbartbinder' (manufacturer of these hats) for one decorative hat which is sold for several thousands of marks.

'Charivari' means a watch chain decorated with enchased teeth of marmot or stag, old coins, tines of an antler and other things.

Buttnmandln

In the Advent, mostly the evening before Saint Nikolaus Day or Santa Claus Day you see the 'Buttnmandln' running through Berchtesgaden, accompanied by Saint Nikolaus. Mostly they are young unmarried guys covered from head to toe in straw, with heavy cow bells on the back, furmasks over their faces and switches in their hands. They usually number twelve and they are headed by Saint Nikolaus. Having been bound in straw in a farmer's barn in the afternoon, the 'Buttnmandln' get together at a certain place, say the Lord's Prayer and leave. Headed by Saint Nikolaus with measured steps the 'Buttnmanndln' run and jump around with the bells rattling loudly. It is weird to meet the wild groups in the dark. Saint Nikolaus praises or criticizes the children and distributes small gifts, the children watch the 'Buttnmanndln' with suspicion and fear.

Top, left: After being bound in straw, only the dreadful mask made of wood to be seen on the picture opposite is missing.

Centre: The 'Weinfelder Buttnmandln' named after the 'Weinfeldhof' (farm) in the barn of which they were bound in straw in the afternoon with Saint Nikolaus and a 'Kramperl' dressed in fur.

Bottom: After a short prayer the 'Buttnmanndln' leave to see the already waiting children. In Berchtesgaden they 'run' rattling their bells on the evening before Saint Nikolaus Day.

The Christmas Rifle Clubs

The riflemen are guys and men who with salute guns or salute cannons fire volleys in the Advent. The clubs are different from any other rifle clubs in German regions and therefore cannot be compared with the clubs in the Bavarian upland. Their tradition is based on religion and predominantly connected with religious holidays. Their shots intensify the sound of the church bells announcing Jesus Christ's birth, the beginning of the New Year or the miracle of Pentecost.

Every 17th December, that is one week before Christmas Eve, the 'Christkindl' (the infant Jesus) is saluted. For the first time the heavy salute guns resound together with the church bells announcing the coming of Christmas. On Christmas Eve the riflemen get together at their usual stands which can be reached by the sound of the church bells. When half an hour before midnight the church bells start to ring to call the people to the Midnight Mass, the Christmas Saluting in its proper sense begins. Valleys and mountains reecho with the salute guns' sound. The sound is caused by independent fire, quick fire or volleys. The shooting lasts until midnight, stops all of a sudden on the dot of midnight when the Midnight Mass begins. The shooting is done to the glory of God, not to be a feast for the eyes and ears of the tourists.

Right: Riflemen beneath the 'Lockstein'.

Bottom: The snow-covered 'Schloßplatz' (castle place). Above, on the left, the artificial star on the 'Lockstein', the usual stand of the 'Untersberg' riflemen.

Carrying palms

Easter time starts on Palm Sunday when the palms are consecrated and the Holy Week is introduced. The palms are branched-out bunches of willows decorated with colourful 'Schaberbandln' (wood shavings) of the length of some inches to one yard, plaited in balls, rings or stars. A bunch of boxtree or cedar is wound around the lowest fork of the bunch, branches of boxtree or cedar added to the mostly thin branches of the willows. Nails or wire must by no means be used. Younger boys, the 'Palmtrager' take the palms to the church where they are consecrated during a mass. After that the 'Palm-trager' takes his palms to the families he knows and gets a small present in return. The palms are put behind the cross and on the fields of farms to ask for God's blessing during the following year.

Left page: Two 'Palmtrager' from Metzenleiten before going the church. The smaller of the two, looking so roguish to the camera, has put together the pictures of this booklet.

Right, top: When climbing the maypoles one has to reach the crown where the most delightful prizes are written down on sheets of paper.

Right, bottom: In order to celebrate the summer bonfires are lit on various summits or in front of different forest huts.

Traditional costumes

'Das G'wand', the traditional clothing belongs to the Berchtesgaden traditions, even if it is not worn as often as it was only a few decades ago, especially by the fair sex.

Men's traditional costumes

Instead of a tie the 'Bindl' is worn to the white shirt with stitched tucks. The pants of tinted brown or black leather are short in summer, without turn-ups and embroidered green, in winter they are longer, bound beneath the knee like breeches and embroidered white. On high religious holidays mostly black long trousers are worn.

The stockings are knitted by hand, bright or dark grey, of knee-length. The shoes, the so-called 'Haferlschuhe' or 'Allgäuer' are stable low shoes tied up at one side. The jacket, the 'Bandljoppe' consists either of a bright grey or a dark grey cloth with short turn-ups and a low stand-up collar. The plain back has a little horizontal strap, the exterior seams are edged with green riibons of 0.8 inch and the turn-ups are decorated by embroidery.

The hat going with it is a broad brimmed green hat, the 'Rundscheibling', slightly pointed in the form of a cone in the middle. The other form of hats is the oval-shaped rifleman's hat pointing downwards at the front rim. Both hats are of dark green velours or felt the middle wound by green ribbons. Different decorations like 'Gamsbart' 'Hirschbart' can be added.

Left page: The popular dance 'Schuhplatteln' is continued by the clubs for the continued use of traditional costumes, both for showing it to foreign people and to one's own delight. The men sometimes release their girls and beat their thigs and shoes with their palms. The strong rhythm of this dance that can easily be changed is another reason of the 'Schuhplattler's popularity.

Right: The Berchtesgaden traditional costume of man in its different forms. So they are worn especially on sundays. Various hats, long black trousers or short leather pants or leather breeches, knee-length stockings or calf stockings (bottom right). There are no modifications of the 'Haferlschuhe', the Berchtesgaden 'Bandljoppe' (jacket) is either bright grey or dark grey.

Women's traditional costumes

The black velvet sleeveless bodice is worn over a white cotton blouse with puffed sleeves, its seams are edged by green ribbons and sometimes it has an embroidered back. The calf-long skirt of black cloth for the sunday dress, otherwise of dark green cloth, measures 4.45 yards at the bottom and its seam is edged with ragged braids.

A neckerchief of silk or wool muslin is worn over the 'Pfoad' (blouse) and the bodice. It is pleated to the form of a triangle one end of which covering the back and the other two ends crossed over the breast. The neckerchief and the apron are of the same cloth, the apron being a little shorter than the skirt.

The Berchtesgaden traditional costumes are not only for holidays, but are mostly by men worn every day. During the week chequered shirts are put on instead of white ones. Other modifications are usual as well because after all the traditional costume is no uniform.

Panorama of the Berchtesgaden area looking southwards. All of the valley basin is surrounded by high mountain massifs, in detail they are: the 'Hoher Göll', the 'Hagengebirge', the 'Steinernes Meer', the 'Hochkalter', the 'Reiteralpe' and the 'Untersberg'. In the form of a heart the border to Austria goes across these mountains. The Watzmann is enthroned above the valley basin and is the only of these mountains that is without the border.

Only three roads lead to Berchtesgaden, namely across Schellenberg, Hallthurm – Bischofswiesen, Schneizlreuth – Wachterl – Ramsau. A fourth path, important in former times, lead to the Pinzgau across the Hirschbichl and nowadays is preserved for pedestrians.

Clockwise the communities of Schönau am Königssee, Ramsau, Bischofswiesen, Schellenberg surround the geographic centre of Markt Berchtesgaden.

» *Wen Gott lieb hat, den läßt er fallen, in dies' Land*«

Ludwig Ganghofer

Whom God loves, He will drop to this land.

*Shortly before sunrise at the cross on the summit of the
'Roßfeld'. Another day in our beautiful area will begin.*